Jane Austen
in 41 Objects

Jane Austen
in 41 Objects

Kathryn Sutherland

JANE
AUSTEN'S
HOUSE

BODLEIAN
LIBRARY
PUBLISHING

For Sophie Reynolds

First published in 2025 by
Bodleian Library Publishing
Broad Street, Oxford OX1 3BG
in association with Jane Austen's House

www.bodleianshop.co.uk

ISBN 978 1 85124 626 7

Images reproduced courtesy of Jane Austen's House,
unless otherwise specified on p. 206

Publisher: Samuel Fanous
Managing Editor: Susie Foster
Editor: Janet Phillips
Picture Editor: Leanda Shrimpton
Cover design by Dot Little at the Bodleian Library
Designed and typeset by Lucy Morton at illuminati in 10½ on 15 ITC New Baskerville
Printed and bound in China by Shenzhen Reliance Printing Co. Ltd.
on 140 gsm Chinese Golden Sun Woodfree paper

British Library Catalogue in Publishing Data
A CIP record of this publication is available from the British Library

Contents

Acknowledgements

My thanks go to all at Bodleian Library Publishing: most especially to Samuel Fanous, Head of Publishing, and to Janet Phillips, Editor, for encouraging me to discover a book in 41 objects; to Leanda Shrimpton, Picture Editor, for her resourcefulness and creative skill in finding and placing images. I am indebted to the wonderful staff at Jane Austen's House, Chawton, where I am Patron: to Lizzie Dunford, Director, for supporting this project so enthusiastically, and to Sophie Reynolds, Head of Collections, Interpretation and Engagement. Sophie has worked alongside me at every stage, searching through the House archives, rooting out provenance, answering my endless questions and supplying images. This book would not exist without her cheerful professionalism and her friendship. My thanks to John and Virginia Murray, whose front door is still open and welcoming; to my sister Moira Wardhaugh for photographs; and to all those who have answered queries and generously shared images and objects with me: Austen family members, librarians and archivists, curators, collectors and fans. Thank you, also, to the anonymous reader of my typescript for keen and sympathetic criticism.

A chronology
of Jane Austen

1764   26 April: marriage of Revd George Austen (1731–1805) and Cassandra Leigh (1739–1827), JA's parents.

1765   13 February: James Austen (1765–1819), JA's eldest brother, born in Deane, Hampshire.

1766   26 August: George Austen (1766–1838) the younger born in Deane.

1767   7 October: Edward Austen (Knight 1812) (1767–1852) born in Deane.

1768   July/August: Austen family move to Steventon Rectory, Hampshire.

1771   8 June: Henry Austen (1771–1850) born in Steventon.

1773   9 January: Cassandra Austen (1773–1845) born in Steventon; boy pupils are boarded at Steventon from now until 1796.

1774   23 April: Francis (Frank) Austen (1774–1865) born in Steventon.

1775   16 December: JA (1775–1817) born in Steventon.

1779   23 June: Charles Austen (1779–1852) born in Steventon.

1781   Marriage of JA's cousin, Eliza Hancock (1761–1813), to Jean-François Capot de Feuillide, in France.

1782   December: Austen family amateur theatricals performed in Steventon.

1783   Edward, JA's third brother, adopted by Mr and Mrs Thomas Knight of Godmersham, Kent; JA, Cassandra and cousin Jane

Cooper tutored by kinswoman Mrs Cawley for some months in Oxford and Southampton until they fall ill, probably with typhus fever; death of aunt Jane Cooper from typhus.

1785–6 JA and Cassandra attend the Abbey House School, Reading.

1787 JA begins writing stories, collected in three notebooks (to 1793).

1787–9 Cousin Eliza de Feuillide visits Steventon; performance there of amateur theatricals, perhaps including dramatic sketches written by JA; cousins Eliza de Feuillide and Philadelphia Walter attend the trial in London of Warren Hastings, impeached for corruption in India.

1789 James and Henry Austen at St John's College, Oxford, produce student periodical *The Loiterer* (to March 1790); JA begins lifelong friendship with Martha Lloyd and sister Mary when their mother rents Deane Parsonage.

1791 Edward Austen marries Elizabeth Bridges.

1792 James Austen marries Anne Mathew.

Winter?: Cassandra becomes engaged to Revd Tom Fowle, former pupil of Revd George Austen.

1793 Birth of eldest nieces, Fanny and Anna, daughters of brothers Edward and James; JA writes last of entries in the teenage notebooks.

1794 JA probably drafting the novella *Lady Susan*; Capot de Feuillide, cousin Eliza's husband, guillotined in Paris.

1795 JA writes 'Elinor and Marianne' (first draft of *Sense and Sensibility*).

May: death of James Austen's wife; his daughter Anna sent to live at Steventon with aunts JA and Cassandra.

December: JA's flirtation with Tom Lefroy over the Christmas holiday period, as recorded in her earliest surviving letter.

1796 January: Tom Lefroy leaves for London; Tom Fowle, Cassandra's fiancé, sails for West Indies.

October: JA begins 'First Impressions' (first draft of *Pride and Prejudice*), finished August 1797; subscribes to Frances Burney's *Camilla*.

1797 January: marriage of Harris Bigg-Wither; Anna returns to live with them.

February: Tom Fowle, Cassandra's fiancé, dies of fever off San Domingo.

1 November: Revd George Austen unsuccessfully offers a novel (perhaps 'First Impressions') to the publisher Cadell; JA rewriting 'Elinor and Marianne' as *Sense and Sensibility*.

November: Mrs Austen takes JA and Cassandra to Bath; Edward Austen takes possession of Godmersham Park, Kent.

31 December: marriage of Henry Austen and cousin Eliza de Feuillide.

1798 JA begins writing 'Susan' (*Northanger Abbey*), set in Bath.

17 November: James's son James Edward, JA's future biographer, born.

1799 The arrest and imprisonment of JA's aunt Mrs Leigh Perrot on a charge of shoplifting.

1800 March: trial and acquittal of Mrs Leigh Perrot.

December: Revd George Austen decides to retire and move to Bath.

1801 Henry Austen sets up as banker and army agent in London.

May: the Austens (Revd and Mrs, Cassandra and Jane) leave Steventon and settle in Bath; first of several seaside holidays in West Country (to 1804), during one of which JA may have had a brief romantic involvement with a man who died shortly afterwards.

1802 2 December: Harris Bigg-Wither, a family friend, proposes to JA, who accepts and then, overnight, rejects his offer; she revises 'Susan'.

1803 Spring: JA sells 'Susan' to Crosby & Co. for £10.

November: the Austens visit Lyme Regis.

1804 Late summer: the Austens holiday in Lyme Regis.

1804–5 JA drafts *The Watsons*; finishes and makes a fair copy of *Lady Susan*.

1805 21 January: death of Revd George Austen, JA's father, in Bath; JA stops working on *The Watsons*; Martha Lloyd joins the Austen household.

18 June: James Austen's youngest child Caroline born in Steventon, in later life a major source of biographical information on her aunt JA.

1806 July: Austen female household leave Bath.

October: they take lodgings in Southampton with Frank Austen and his new wife.

1807 March: Austen female household move into house in Castle Square, Southampton.

1808 JA visits Godmersham; death of Edward Austen's wife Elizabeth after giving birth to eleventh child.

1809 5 April: JA attempts unsuccessfully to make Crosby & Co. publish 'Susan', writing under pseudonym 'Mrs Ashton Dennis' ('M.A.D.').

July: Austen female household move into Chawton Cottage, in the village of Chawton, Hampshire, owned by brother Edward.

1810 Winter: *Sense and Sensibility* accepted for publication by Thomas Egerton.

1811 February: JA planning *Mansfield Park*.

March–April: JA stays with Henry and Eliza in London to correct proofs of *Sense and Sensibility*.

30 October: *Sense and Sensibility* published on commission; Winter?: JA revising 'First Impressions' as *Pride and Prejudice*.

1812 October: death of Mrs Thomas Knight; Edward Austen and family officially take name of Knight.

November: JA sells copyright of *Pride and Prejudice* to Egerton for £110.

1813 28 January: *Pride and Prejudice* published to acclaim; JA in London to nurse Eliza.

25 April: Eliza dies.

July?: JA finishes *Mansfield Park*; July, first instalment of *Pride and Prejudice* published in French in Geneva-based periodical *La Bibliothèque Britannique*.

October: second editions of *Sense and Sensibility* and *Pride and Prejudice*.

1814 21 January: JA begins *Emma*.

March: visits brother Henry in London, and again in August and November.

9 May: Egerton publishes *Mansfield Park* on commission; it sells out in six months.

8 November: marriage of niece Anna Austen to Ben Lefroy.

1815 29 March: *Emma* finished.

8 August: JA begins *Persuasion*.

October: JA in London nursing Henry, who is ill, and seeing *Emma* through the press.

13 November: JA visits the Prince Regent's library at Carlton House; JA invited to dedicate *Emma* to Prince Regent; *Sense and Sensibility* is published in French as *Raison et sensibilité* (further French translations of JA's novels in 1816, 1821, 1822, 1824).

23 December: *Emma* published (dated 1816) by fashionable publisher John Murray.

1816 February: second edition of *Mansfield Park* published by Murray; Henry buys back the manuscript of 'Susan', which JA revises as 'Catherine'.

15 March: failure of Henry's bank and he leaves London.

Spring: JA's health begins to fail.

18 July: first draft of *Persuasion* finished.

6 August: *Persuasion* finally completed.

December: Henry ordained as Anglican priest and becomes curate of Chawton; *Emma* published in America (Philadelphia).

1817 27 January–18 March: JA at work on *Sanditon*.

28 March: death of James Leigh Perrot, JA's uncle.

27 April: JA makes her will.

24 May: Cassandra takes JA to Winchester for medical attention.

18 July: JA dies in early morning.

24 July: JA buried in Winchester Cathedral; third edition of *Pride and Prejudice*.

20 December: *Northanger Abbey* and *Persuasion* published together (dated 1818) by Murray, with Henry Austen's 'Biographical Notice of the Author', the first official notice in print of JA's authorship of the novels.

1819   James Austen, JA's eldest brother, dies.

1827   Mrs Austen, JA's mother, dies.

1828   Frank Austen marries his second wife Martha Lloyd.

1832–3   *Elizabeth Bennet; or, Pride and Prejudice* (and the other novels) published in America (Philadelphia); Murray considers a collected edition of JA's novels.

1833   Bentley's collected edition of JA's novels (frequently reprinted until 1882, the Steventon Edition); Henry Austen's revised 'Memoir of Miss Austen' prefixed to *Sense and Sensibility*.

1837   James Edward Austen, JA's nephew, takes name of Leigh.

1843   9 May: Cassandra Austen executes her will, adding a testamentary letter distributing her possessions, among which are JA's manuscripts.

1845   22 March: Cassandra Austen dies; JA's manuscripts and letters are divided among the family.

1850   Henry Austen dies.

1852   Edward Austen Knight dies; Charles Austen dies.

1864   Anna Lefroy writes down her 'Recollections of Aunt Jane'.

1865   Sir Francis Austen dies, the last of JA's remaining siblings.

1867   Caroline Austen writes 'My Aunt Jane Austen: A Memoir' (only published in 1952).

1869   16 December: *A Memoir of Jane Austen* (dated 1870), by her nephew James Edward Austen-Leigh, the first major biography, incorporating the recollections of his sisters Anna and Caroline. From its publication stems JA's rising popularity through the rest of the nineteenth century.

1871   Second edition of *Memoir*, with *Lady Susan*, *The Watsons*, the cancelled chapter of *Persuasion*, and extracts from the unfinished *Sanditon*.

1872 Brass memorial tablet placed in Winchester Cathedral by James Edward Austen-Leigh, from the proceeds of the *Memoir*; Anna Lefroy dies.

1874 James Edward Austen-Leigh dies.

1880 Caroline Austen dies.

1884 *Letters of Jane Austen*, edited by her great-nephew Lord Brabourne, the first attempt to collect her correspondence.

1900 Memorial window erected to JA in Winchester Cathedral, paid for by public subscription.

1902 *Jane Austen: Her Homes and Her Friends*, by Constance Hill, with drawings by Ellen Hill, a significant non-family biography, based on interviews, manuscript records and illustrations of sites subsequently destroyed.

1913 *Life and Letters of Jane Austen*, by W. and R.A. Austen-Leigh, JA's great-nephew and great-great-nephew, published (the basis of Deirdre Le Faye's authoritative biography, *Jane Austen, A Family Record*, 2nd edn, 2004).

1917 A plaque, designed by Ellen Hill, placed on Chawton Cottage to mark the 100th anniversary of JA's death.

1922 JA's second notebook of teenage stories published as *Love & Freindship* (followed by the first notebook in 1933 and the third in 1951).

1940 The Jane Austen Society founded.

1947 Chawton Cottage, Hampshire, JA's last home, purchased as a permanent museum by the Jane Austen Memorial Trust.

1949 July: Jane Austen's House opens to the public.

1979 Jane Austen Society of North America founded.

1989 Jane Austen Society of Australia founded.

1995 Andrew Davies's BBC television mini-series of *Pride and Prejudice* is a significant landmark in JA's popularity, marking her promotion to multi-media stardom.

2017 September: JA becomes the face of the Bank of England £10 note.

Introduction
A life in objects

Imagine a life story as a house clearance—that's how for many of us it finds shape, as objects are passed on, memories stirred and made. Some objects will be bequests, handed down in the family or between friends; others will be sold. Yet others will make their way into charity shops, to find new owners and make new stories. Some will be thrown out. Imagine, if you can, the most unencumbered, uncluttered, twenty-first-century Western woman's life: by comparison with Jane Austen's, it will be rich in possessions. She owned very little in her own right: clothing, of course—gowns, coats, shawls, shoes, undergarments, many of which were, over time, repaired and adapted to reflect changes in fashion; modest pieces of costume jewellery; books; a piano.[1] Some of these items have survived to the present day, preserved in museum and family collections. Others have long since lost all connection to their famous owner, and some have left no trace. This is Jane Austen's life as recorded in objects.

The story begins in the summer of 1768, seven years before Jane Austen's birth. Mrs Cassandra Austen is making the short journey from Deane to her new home in Steventon, Hampshire, lying inelegantly on top of a mattress in a waggon filled with household goods. Her husband, the Revd George Austen, has insured the waggon's contents for £300. Mrs Austen, the mother of three sons, may once again be pregnant; if so, she will lose the child.[2] The next to be born will be her fourth son, Henry, in 1771, followed by a daughter, Cassandra, in 1773, a further son, Francis (known in the family as Frank), in 1774, and Jane, in 1775. Her final child will be Charles in 1779. The route the heavily loaded waggon travels is, in 1768, no more than a cart track, rutted and pitted with holes after persistent summer rains, and impassable for most vehicles. That so much circumstantial detail of the removal has survived in family anecdote suggests how etched its discomfort was in Mrs Austen's memory. The journey may indeed have resulted in painful loss.

What we don't have is an account of the domestic items that accompanied the move. Leaving Steventon for Bath thirty-three years later, the Austens auctioned most of their house contents. Advertisements appearing in the local newspaper, the *Reading Mercury*, on 20 and 27 April and 4 May 1801, help us reconstruct the interior of Jane Austen's earliest home, the place where she was born and lived until the age of twenty-five. As well as the expected bedsteads, bedding, chests of drawers, chairs and carpets, the sale included pier glasses, a mahogany sideboard, a 'modern set of circular dining tables', Pembroke and card tables, a pianoforte together with a collection of music books, a terrestrial globe and microscope, two bookcases, 200 volumes of books, Wedgwood tableware, an eight-day clock, a side of bacon, some kitchen, dairy and brewing utensils and a set of theatrical scenes. The auction was held over three days, from 5 to 7 May. The Revd Austen's farm stock was disposed of in a separate sale.[3]

The piano was a Ganer and belonged to Jane. It fetched 8 guineas, 'about what I really expected to get' she recorded in a letter of 12 May, adding 'I am more anxious to know the amount of my books, especially as they are said to have sold well.' But 'only Eleven Guineas for the Tables' was a 'blow'.[4] The globe and microscope were perhaps relics of the rectory schoolroom where the Revd Austen prepared boy boarders for university entrance. Wedgwood breakfast and dinner services, like the piano, were replaced when, from 1809, the Austen women established a home at Chawton. The theatrical scenery recalls the family's private dramatics of the 1780s and early 1790s when James, the eldest son, wrote prologues and epilogues, and children and adults acted plays in the Steventon barn with their cousins and neighbours, perhaps including in their repertoire some of Jane's own teenage sketches. If the Austens used painted stage sets, their productions were quite elaborate.

In the brief will she drew up on 27 April 1817, only months before her death, Jane Austen left the bulk of her most valuable assets (the profits and copyrights from her novels) to her sister Cassandra.[5] Before her first novel was published in 1811, at the age of thirty-five, she had no income of her own. A small legacy of £50 in 1806 is described as sufficient to meet her expenses for a year.[6] The profits from novels not ploughed into underwriting costs for the next publication were invested in 'Navy Fives', government bonds yielding 5 per cent interest a year, issued to fund the Royal Navy. Her purchase, possibly in spring 1815, of £600-worth of stocks brought an annual £30.[7] She never owned a house or a carriage, and for most things was dependent on her father and, after his death in 1805, her brothers.

Such dependency was social as well as economic: as a gentlewoman she could not travel any distance unescorted; she could only enjoy the amusements that London had to offer thanks to brother Henry, who lived there. At the same time, she belonged to a quickening consumer society, dominated as is ours by material goods and services. Late Georgian and Regency England saw an increase in home comforts, from furnishings and domestic appliances to luxury foods; shopping (a term in use alongside 'marketing' only from the mid-eighteenth century) was by now an amusement as much as a necessity. Libraries, public lecture rooms, museums, picture galleries, concert halls offered opportunities for women to mix in public and for self-improvement. But social spaces and arrangements, within and outside the home, were gendered along lines that were fixed, and in some instances remained so far into the twentieth century.

An early letter, written 28 December 1798, to her sister Cassandra, on an extended visit to brother Edward at Godmersham Park in Kent, includes the detail: 'If you will send my father an account of your Washing & Letter expences &c, he will send You a draft for the amount of it, as well as for your next quarter, & for Edward's Rent.'[8] The Revd Austen's Hoare's bank account shows that he sent £12 19*s* 6*d*.[9] On this occasion Cassandra stayed at Godmersham for around seven months. Elizabeth, Edward's wife, was expecting their fifth child in a little under seven years; she would die in October 1808 soon after the birth of an eleventh. Unmarried women of Austen's rank needed to prove themselves serviceable to married kin and their families. During Elizabeth's all too frequent pregnancies, Cassandra was the indispensable spinster aunt, managing the household, helping with the education of those children still at home, making clothes. This was unpaid work.

Dependent gentlewomen, as Austen's surviving correspondence makes clear, included in their expected duties sustaining kinship ties through social visits, writing family letters (the main conduits of news) and supplicating people of influence for career advancement for their men. In addition, they preserved their social standing, even in the face of personal hardship, through charitable service and donations. They were not idle, but their activities have left little trace. 'For very little is known about women ... Often nothing tangible remains of a woman's day', Virginia Woolf wrote in 1929, adding the comment: 'Where does the accent fall?'[10] Underestimated then and now, the energy-sapping restraint imposed by genteel domesticity upon women's aspirations and actions 'effectively inhibited other ways of life'.[11] It is one of the remarkable facts about Jane Austen that out of circumstances of relative powerlessness and the tedium of daily obligation and confinement to 'the lesser duties of life', as she describes them in *Sense and Sensibility* (ch. 46), she transformed the novel into the most powerful vehicle for female expression.

Owning little, she practised thrift in drawing attention to objects in her adult fictions. Not so in the teenage stories, where things out of place regularly breach the ordinary even to the verge of nonsensical surreality: the large Newfoundland dog sent once a month as a gift into Warwickshire; aristocratic dinner tables loaded with the coarsest foods—cow heels, tripe and giblets; the gold watch whose extravagant purchase leads Eliza Cecil's children to bite off two of her fingers to stave off starvation.[12] The critic Barbara Hardy noted half a century ago how, after *Sense and Sensibility*, *Pride and Prejudice* and *Mansfield Park*, Austen moved in her later novels 'to the significance of smaller and more shifting things', portable possessions rather than the character-defining property of landed estates and big houses, to show the connection between an 'inner self' and its 'outer case'.

Small things can be almost sacred, as is Fanny Price's 'nest of comforts', assembled out of bits and pieces in the old schoolroom at Mansfield Park—a faded footstool, a collection of family silhouettes, a sketch of her brother's ship; objects none of which is considered good enough for display elsewhere (ch. 16). Or they can be slippery, unnoticed clues—in *Emma*, the spectacles whose loose rivet Frank Churchill is discovered mending with such fixed concentration in Miss Bates's sitting room (ch. 28). The silver knife, relic of little dead Mary, over which Fanny's sisters quarrel (*Mansfield Park*, ch. 38), is a disturbing accessory amid Portsmouth's squalor. Though, like Fanny's amber cross, it possibly derives from something actual, an object Austen too may have lingered over: 'has she a silver knife', she enquires of Cassandra, 30 June 1808, anxious to provide an appropriate gift.[13] In *Persuasion*, caught out by rain when walking in Bath, the comparative thickness of Anne Elliot's boots is a topic to be dwelt on; Lady Russell staring through the carriage window is discovered to be watching out for a particular pair of curtains in a house across the road and not, as Anne supposes, for a glimpse of Captain Wentworth (ch. 19); during the musical evening in the Upper Assembly Rooms, Anne and Mr Elliot hold between them a concert programme from which she explains the words of an Italian song (ch. 20). Hardy concluded from such stubborn materiality that 'things take a hand in human destiny', and that though she resists 'symbolic manipulation of things', 'the intimate connection of things with their owners and donors is more personal in Jane Austen than in any other novelist before her, and perhaps after her too.'[14]

There is, also, something compensatory in a regard for faded footstools, thick boots and window curtains. Mundane objects link Austen the novelist to the letter writer whose fixing upon 'little matters', as she describes them to Cassandra, 18 April 1811,[15] turns the emptiness of the female day—having nothing significant to say (a common refrain in her letters of obligation)—into fruitful watchfulness and a kind of redemption through random detail: 'not being overburdened with subject—(having nothing at all to say)—I shall have no check to my Genius from beginning to end', she wrote 21 January 1801.[16] Accordingly, 'I am still a Cat if I see a Mouse'.[17] A woman's letters, literally, are spaces to be filled, like household cupboards or drawers, and nothing that furnishes this end is wasted:

'You know how interesting the purchase of a sponge-cake is to me.'[18] The disconnected 'nothings' of Austen's domestic correspondence can take on the appearance of an inventory of the day's passing moments. The domestic letter was her model for fiction, the shadow life of her novels. In her hands, the transfiguring challenge of the realist novel begins with the domestic letter: how and what do you write when you have so little to say?

Structurally deeper than this is the injunction that genteel society placed on women to monitor their conduct—to watch one another and to account for their own time. Highlighting 'Austen's talent for surveillance', Carol Houlihan Flynn locates her 'at the centre of a tradition both literary and domestic which requires that the female figure be always ready for inspection'.[19] Such inspection included a thorough knowledge of the contents of a wardrobe. Flynn reaches her conclusion from a letter in which Austen—reporting, 30 November 1814, to her niece Fanny Knight on a visit she has made to another niece, Anna, newly married—writes: 'I certainly could describe her bed-room, & her Drawers & her Closet … Her purple Pelisse rather surprised me … I suspect nothing worse than its' being got in secret, & not owned to anybody.—She is capable of that you know.'[20] Was Austen invited by Anna to inspect the inside of her closet and her recent purchases or was she snooping—a stealthy commentator on another's suspected stealth in breaking those unwritten rules governing female behaviour by purchasing an inappropriately purple pelisse? In such instances, objects bear witness.

Objects can summon up a life, can provide a glimpse into something remote or surprisingly near, something alternative. They cling and create attachments, give colour and depth, bring someone into temporary focus and relate them to others. Jane Austen was a materialist, defined by patterns and habits of consumption that exhibited and re-enforced her social status, her sense of self and her place in the world. Her characters move through rooms filled with hard and soft furnishings; they know price and value. The opening chapters of *Sense and Sensibility*, her first published novel, provide a lesson as Mr and Mrs John Dashwood, Norland's inheritors, whittle down the amount it is reasonable to bestow on the widow and her three daughters they are about to render homeless: £3,000 to be settled on the girls soon resolves into 'the china, plate, and linen' already their mother's by right. Even then, the breakfast china is a topic of regret as far too good for a female household of reduced means. In a novel whose opening scenes are sharply reminiscent of the downturn in the fortunes of the Austen women post-1805, wider wellbeing might indeed be registered in cups and saucers and the fate of the family plate. In *Persuasion*, her last published novel, the 'grand piano forte and a harp, flower-stands and little tables placed in every direction' intrude unwelcome modernity upon the 'order and neatness' of the 'old-fashioned square parlour' at the Great House, Uppercross, marking out the Musgroves as a family 'in a state of alteration' (ch. 5). Generational shifts are gathered inside a taste in furniture, and small household objects carry the historical charge of a world order which in 1815, the year of *Persuasion*'s writing, was itself undergoing profound transition.

Austen's was, as ours is, a world of things. The front pages of national newspapers, a good indicator of social preoccupations in her media age, were filled with advertisements and notices of things for sale or rent, from houses to cut-price cloth, fruit trees, books and japan blacking.[21] Objects remain solid and tangible in her fictions, even where they appear to take on more symbolic or subjective associations, as with Fanny Price's amber cross and chain. In literary terms, we might say that her approach is metonymic rather than metaphoric; that Austen's objects do not blur or soften in light of their spiritual or abstract functions but retain their hard edges. This is perhaps especially the case when she writes at her most romantic, in this scene from *Pride and Prejudice*, for example: 'Will you tell me how long you have loved him?' Jane Bennet enquires; and her sister Elizabeth replies: 'It has been coming on so gradually, that I hardly know when it began. But I believe I must date it from my first seeing his beautiful grounds at Pemberley' (ch. 59). Mr Darcy's estate, the large, handsome country house, rolling wooded parklands and his £10,000 a year really do matter. In an early study of the novel form, Dorothy Van Ghent observed that the 'general directions of reference taken by Austen's language … are clearly materialistic', reflecting the culture of her own commercial society with its base, much like ours, in 'acquisitiveness and calculation and materialism'. It is this 'single materialistic language' that, according to Van Ghent, Austen 'forces—or blandishes or intrigues—into spiritual duties', through antithesis, irony and direct and indirect play.[22] Put another way, romance is in service to worldliness. Especially since the mid-1990s and her explosion onto the screen, her romantic vision of sexual love has assumed a seemingly unassailable status as the sum total of her fiction. Yet she herself was an outsider where romance was concerned—sharp-eyed to its likely conclusion. Reality may be redeemed for her heroine but for few others. Her own fate was uncomfortably closer to that of *Emma*'s Miss Bates, middle-aged unmarried daughter of a clergyman, grateful for gifts of sacks of apples and game birds in season or half a Stilton cheese.[23] Romance, though, she well knew sells books.

❧

Jane Austen's writing emerged from a dynamic space that was domestic and ordinary. The visible and known lives of gentry women either much like herself or within her acquaintance offered prompts to the imagination. It is the domestic interior and its extension the garden that give Austen and her heroines an equivalent to what the Romantic poets find in exterior landscape: a private retreat. But her houses and gardens are ambiguous spaces and hers a privacy hard won from the sociable obligations that domesticity imposes on women. The life built inside a few rooms could also be imprisoning. In her day, only the bedroom was a truly private space, and even then not always; she and sister Cassandra shared a bedroom for much of their lives. At Chawton Cottage, the double dining room and sitting room were both family and public spaces for wider entertaining. She had no writing room that was not also a social space open to intrusion. Beginning or resuming a letter, she sometimes describes as a luxury finding herself alone in a room in which to write: 'very snug, in my own room', on a visit to Godmersham, 6 November 1813; 'writing by myself at the new Table in the front room', in Henrietta Street, London, 2 March 1814; and, after breakfast, with 'the room to myself again', at Hans Place, London, 24 August 1814.[24] In Austen's fiction, there is a balance to seek between the dual interior spaces in which her characters move: between the object-filled drawing room and that other inner space, the life of the mind; between architectural and psychological interiors; between objectivity and subjectivity. Austen's heroines, in particular, offer the reader models for living inside the house and inside oneself.

In *The Sense of an Interior: Four Writers and the Rooms that Shaped Them,* Diana Fuss asks us to make connections between the act of creativity and the spaces that might hold it. Her focus is the writer's room: in her case, the rooms of Emily Dickinson, Sigmund Freud, Helen Keller and Marcel Proust. She describes these rooms as mutable ground and argues for a two-way interaction that deserves serious attention: 'the creative act of composition poses its own physical challenges, while the built environment offers up a store of metaphysical questions'.[25] The writer's room exerts a more extensive influence upon artistic vision than is represented solely by its architectural bounds, its walls and windows or the disposition of a desk. Austen wrote in the domestic space of a family parlour that was never hers alone. For her, the private space of imagining is also always the sociable space for living. She left no account, but her nephew biographer remembered a small writing table set by the window and a door whose hinges went unoiled so that the creaky noise of its opening would alert her to intrusion:

> she had no separate study to retire to, and most of the work
> must have been done in the general sitting-room, subject to
> all kinds of casual interruptions. She was careful that her
> occupation should not be suspected by servants, or visitors, or
> any persons beyond her own family party. She wrote upon small
> sheets of paper which could easily be put away, or covered with
> a sheet of blotting paper. There was, between the front door
> and the offices, a swing door which creaked when it was opened;
> but she objected to having this little inconvenience remedied,
> because it gave her notice when anyone was coming.[26]

Whether history or myth, the creaking door marks the threshold between art and life. Another account, from a niece, tells how 'her desk lived in the drawing room. I often saw her writing letters on it, and I beleive she wrote much of her Novels in the same way—sitting with her family, when they were quite alone; but *I* never saw any manuscript of *that* sort, in progress.'[27] Austen's walnut writing table once more sits in the family room in Chawton Cottage, now a museum. Her desk (a mahogany writing box) is in the British Library. In museum space and time, there is something theatrical about the little table's appearance—the room is dressed, reassembled to enforce an acknowledged truth about her writing.

The woman's novel has long been predicated upon the delicate art of living in enclosed spaces. Austen is a novelist who persistently maps space. Though her novels are rarely topographically detailed, her characters find themselves in space. Edward Said's description of *Mansfield Park*, Austen's third novel, as being 'very precisely about a series of both small and large dislocations and relocations in space' might be applied to all her novels. Said was drawing attention to something important in Austen's technique, commenting: 'After Lukács and Proust, we have become so accustomed to thinking of the novel's plot and structure as constituted mainly by temporality that we have overlooked the function of space.'[28] Austen's spaces can be both precisely delineated and psychologically suggestive—assuming heightened significance through an insistent observation that is sometimes emotionally discomforting and at other times just intrusively physical. She is good at defamiliarizing space. In her early fragment novel *The Watsons*, written in 1805, hyper-attention to the layout of rooms at the town ball renders space both physically and mentally odd: characters are hemmed in by furniture they must navigate in order to move from the ballroom into the tea room, which, we are told, was 'a small room within the Card room'. In *Mansfield Park*, Fanny Price, dislocated from her modest Portsmouth home, finds the Mansfield rooms 'too large for her to move in with ease' (ch. 2). Once she has been acclimatized to grander surroundings, 'the smallness of the house, and thinness of the walls', on her return to Portsmouth, 'brought every thing so close to her, that ... she hardly knew how to bear it' (ch. 38). In an early letter, 27 October 1800, Austen commented on the design oddity of a certain Mr Deedes' house, Sandling Park, Kent, that contained 'the very remarkable

& singular feature of a fireplace with a window … exactly over the mantlepeice'.[29]

Austen's writing room, the family parlour, measures 5.3 × 3.9 metres (17⅓ × 12¾ feet). As the daily living space for four women, a space filled with domestic furniture and used for entertaining visitors, it is not difficult to imagine its objects and functions, its sounds and movement, bearing upon the lives of her fictional heroines. Continuing his description of this room, Austen-Leigh wrote:

> In that well occupied female party there must have been many precious hours of silence during which the pen was busy at the little mahogany writing-desk … I, and my sisters and cousins … frequently disturbed this mystic process, without any idea of the mischief that we were doing.

And, extending to her compositions the nineteenth-century belief that the writer's room bears witness to her genius, he commented that her novels 'are like photographs … all is the unadorned reflection of the natural object'—as if material space and imaginary space might be identifiably one.[30] Photo-journalism was already by the 1870s, when he wrote, in use to manufacture public images of writers from the decor and objects among which they lived.

Peel away the mythologizing, used by her nephew to deflect attention from something as socially disruptive as female literary creativity, and his emphasis upon the porous boundary between the built environment and the imagined nevertheless holds true for aspects of Austen's innovatory narrative style. The writing room, which was also the family room, does provide the scene and major ingredients for the novels—and not just all that tea drinking and gossip. Austen is the first great conversational novelist in English, exploiting in fiction the twinned conversability and claustrophobia of domestic space with its audible and overlapping patterns of speaking and being seen to speak. The dilemma the family room posed for the writer is shared by her heroines, each of whom is a creative consciousness. How to carve out private space within sociable space/an inner life that escapes the outer rituals, the constant chatter? Austen's other great contribution to the development of the English novel, the hybrid idiom of free indirect discourse, is born from the need to reach accommodation between inner and outer realities, between privacy and surveillance. The family sitting room conditions her heroines, hemmed in by domestic routine and duty, their every gesture tracked by watching eyes. Through cramped and shared space we reach the private conversation of the self with the self, inner consciousness—Austen's liberating gift to her confined heroines and to the novel.

⚜

How might objects help us imagine a life? To propose a life in a number of objects is to engage, however lightly, the materialist philosophy of the times in which Austen lived, a set of beliefs that we might loosely call environmental psychology, according to which things shape the mind and give rise to our understanding of identity. Through our interactions with things, we find and make ourselves. Early female educationalists, among them Austen's contemporaries Anna Laetitia Barbauld and Maria Edgeworth, argued the importance of object lessons, through the sensations that objects evoke, in teaching children. Many of Edgeworth's stories for children rest upon material specimens, like the objects to be found and inspected inside the drawers of 'the India Cabinet' in 'Rosamond', in *Continuations of Early Lessons* (1814). As stories like 'The Purple Jar' and 'The Birthday Present' suggest, Edgeworth's children are busy little capitalists with a sociable relationship to objects, turning the world cheerfully into consumer desirables and meaning. Nearer our own time, the anthropologist Arjun Appadurai has written of the 'social life' of things, meaning the 'human and social contexts' observable from studying things as they move through the world.[31] Things, objects, by this way of thinking, define our social associations and our value; identity begins with things. Recently, the political theorist Jane Bennett has located something she calls 'vibrant matter', inside a complex ecology in which people and things exchange properties, writing of 'the curious ability of inanimate things to animate, to act, to produce effects dramatic and subtle'. She refers to this as 'thing power'.[32] Eighteenth-century 'it-narratives', popular tales following the fortunes of an object as it circulates in society—the adventures of a banknote, a pair of shoes, a pin—animate the relationship between people and things and suggest that things, too, have a lifecycle that can be expressed as stories.[33]

Closer to the topic of this book, Marilyn Butler described how, in *Northanger Abbey* and the novels of Austen's contemporaries, the 'sophisticated treatment' of 'commodities' as 'signs' to be read and interpreted marks a 'shift in representational style'. She observed: 'Austen involves herself, by allowing the worth of so many of her characters to be quantified for us by things they have bought.'[34] Mrs Allen, Catherine Morland's chaperone in Bath, delights in fabrics; 'dress', we are told, 'was her passion' (ch. 2). General Tilney has filled his medieval abbey home with all the latest conveniences and luxuries—its furniture 'in all the profusion and elegance of modern taste', the kitchen garden 'a village of hot-houses', yielded a hundred pineapples the previous year—and he offers exaggerated apologies for the fact that his elegant Wedgwood breakfast set is now two years old (chs 20, 22). The reader might be forgiven for assuming from these two examples of foolish and unpleasant humanity that consumerist display is under attack in the novel. It would be more accurate to describe it as under examination, a key to the estimation of character. *Northanger Abbey* reminds us that book-reading and book-buying are consumerist choices too. The period saw a rapid growth in publishing of all kinds; the popular Gothic novels of horror and intrigue that colour Catherine's encounters with reality may be read, we are told, 'with great pleasure' by intelligent people (ch. 14). Henry Tilney, Austen's most playful hero, whose boast it is that he has read 'hundreds and hundreds' of novels, enlists Edgeworth-style object lessons to open Catherine's eyes to a truer understanding of the behaviour of those around her. Early on, in a version of learning through play, he draws an analogy between an agreement to dance and the marriage contract (ch. 10); later, he quizzes Catherine's admission that she has 'learnt to love a hyacinth', commenting 'who can tell … you may in time come to love a rose', before concluding that 'The mere habit of learning to love is the thing' (ch. 22). Henry is something of a 'thing theorist' or materialist thinker.

Jane Austen was an enthusiastic shopper, as her letters regularly attest. Things gave her pleasure and, on occasion, she delighted in the idea that the feeling was reciprocated: that things, too, enjoyed her ownership. In her letters objects become animate: on 8 November 1800, after rearrangement of the Steventon rectory furniture, a 'little Table … has most conveniently taken itself off' while others 'send their best Love'; on 23 January 1817 she tells her niece Caroline that the piano, much loved by both of them, 'talks of you;—in various keys, tunes & expressions I allow—but be it Lesson or Country dance, Sonata or Waltz, <u>You</u> are really its' constant Theme'; on 14 March 1817, again to Caroline, the piano sends 'Duty, & will be happy to see you whenever you can come'; on 18 December 1798 she holds a conversation with a bonnet.[35] In an alarming reversal, people can be drained of animation and seemingly become mute domestic fixtures:

Susan Price replacing Fanny as 'the stationary niece' in *Mansfield Park* (ch. 48); Anne Elliot, who, in *Persuasion*, is 'nobody with either father or sister' (ch. 1), is crawled over like an item of furniture by her nephew (ch. 9), and, on another occasion, becomes mere fingers 'mechanically at work' at the piano while others dance (ch. 8). Austen herself was relegated to object status by a literary rival, Mary Russell Mitford, who reported a friend's description of a woman 'no more regarded in society than a poker or a fire-screen, or any other thin upright piece of wood or iron that fills its corner in peace and quietness'.[36] Elsewhere, there is a particular moral aptness in linking possessions to their possessor: in *Emma*, Harriet Smith's box of 'Most precious treasures' contains only a small piece of court plaister and a pencil stub (ch. 40). The triviality is both theirs and hers.

Biography, as Adam Phillips puts it, answers our desire to possess another.[37] Objects are the most tangible signs of possession. As the furnishings of the worlds in which we all move, they familiarize us one to another—help us get a handle, as we say, on someone. Objects can speak eloquently of past lives and of life passing. The relationship is both real and imaginary—a real connection (a fragment of life preserved for posterity) and a point of imaginative departure. To imagine Jane Austen in a series of objects is to intercept their lives at the moment that best reveals hers—the moment when we might almost reach out and touch her. The objects chosen here are to some extent arbitrary, as is the discipline of describing each in around 600 words. Selectivity and partiality define our encounters with other lives; the lives of much loved figures like Jane Austen are no exception. Despite her short life, Jane Austen has led many different lives, and hers is a life still growing and changing, in cultural memory and in unexpected places. This, then, is a biography of Jane Austen discovered aslant through small biographies of things—objects with their own histories, their distinct materialities, that offer shifting entry points into and varying ways of inspecting her life and her afterlives. Each object invites us to meet Jane Austen at a particular moment in her journey from anonymity to literary icon. Each object asks us to acknowledge a reciprocal relation between subject and object, self and thing. We meet them as actors in her life. As Appadurai points out, 'though from a theoretical point of view human actors encode things with significance, from a methodological point of view it is the thing-in-motion that illuminates their human and social contexts.'[38] Jane Austen becomes, in effect, a moment in the life of these objects.

Some of the 41 objects described here belonged to her and cling to our recreation of her like ghostly props: the teenage notebook proudly inscribed 'Volume the First', an early self-pledge of authorship fondly reopened with nieces and nephew years later, a successful published novelist; the costly silk pelisse, a close-fitting garment that summons the absent body it once held, a measure, too, of modest wealth and confidence at a particular moment when life was good. Some are domestic furnishings, in daily use and taken for granted: the dining-room grate in Chawton Cottage, where she prepared tea and toast; the locked tea caddy whose key she kept by her; the unsteady twelve-sided tripod table upon which she set her mahogany writing box; the wallpaper that made the leafy backdrop to her writing. All are powerful imaginative triggers like those Sylvia Plath described after a visit to the Brontë Parsonage at Haworth:

> The black stone rectory rooms of memorabilia—wooden cradle, Charlotte's bridal crown of heirloom lace & honeysuckle, Emily's death couch, the small, luminous books & water-colors, the beaded napkin ring, the Apostle cupboard. They touched this, wore that, wrote here in a house redolent with ghosts.[39]

The theatre bill for the performance at Covent Garden on 15 September 1813 never passed through her hands but provides rare circumstantial evidence for her presence at a particular place—the tangible witness to an intangible experience, forever gone. Some of the objects are places she knew, like the Octagon Room, Bath, and the Cobb, Lyme Regis—real locations. Austen's fictional recreations have taken them out of time and space, transforming them into sites of pilgrimage within the imagined topography of Austen-land. The sermon scrap and the handcrafted Danish translation of *Pride and Prejudice* witness the powerful author-love she early inspired, while the Charleston dinner plate, Mr Darcy's shirt and the Grayson Perry pot represent her abundant and various afterlives in the cultural psyche.

Objects included here situate Austen in Steventon and Chawton, in London, Bath, Dorset and Winchester; they link her to America, India, New Zealand and Europe. Around half the items described belong to or, more accurately, are now housed in Chawton Cottage. Since 1949 the cottage has been reimagined as Jane Austen's House, a writer's house. The writer's house lays a special charm over its contents. With the paraphernalia of mundane domesticity, of tables, chairs and bookcases, of crockery and clothing exhibited as memorials in the space she once lived and worked within, the sense deepens that each item has something particular to say about the writer's life. The very fabric of the house—its bricks and mortar—can cast a spell: like the small piece of wainscot and plaster removed from the Chawton family parlour during restoration and given by the novelist and founding Jane Austen Society member Elizabeth Jenkins to Austen biographer John Halperin in September 1981. When returned to Jane Austen's House in 2019, after Halperin's death, it had been encapsulated, a veritable relic, inside a transparent acrylic block.

With a museum object, we access a reality and a fantasy, some-thing fixed (even frozen) in time and also available for new im-agining. Nicola J. Watson addresses the point in comparing the limited affectiveness of Austen's writing desk or box, held in the British Library, with that of the little writing table, standing by the window in the Chawton parlour. Though the box, a survivor from her late teens, is authentic, the likely repository of her manuscripts and letters, and when opened providing the slope on which she wrote, the writing table exerts the greater pull for visitors as a consequence of its location. As Watson sums it up: 'the imaginative deficit between Austen's table and Austen's writing desk is produced by the desire to locate the scene of writing "at home"; that is, within a simulacrum of the lived domesticity that once generated writing.'[40] Exhibited in the far different heritage space of the British Library, the writing box lacks this lively power. We might say that objects in the right place move us; that, out of place, their significance is harder to register.

Laid out as words and images, 41 objects are to biography what a photograph album is to film—fugitive snapshots, moments in time, rather than a life that flows and is shaped into coherence. Our own lives and the lives of those we encounter testify to something random and shifting—lived discontinuously and unharmoniously with the ticking clock. 'Were I a writer, and dead', Roland Barthes wrote, 'how I would love it if my life, through the pains of some friendly and detached biographer, were to reduce itself to a few details, a few preferences, a few inflections.'[41] Was the artificial flower spray, found in the rafters of Chawton Cottage, hers? Perhaps not; but she knew others like it. The uncooperative odds and ends of the house clear-ance come to mind. These are swift and partial portraits, minimal, fragmentary sketches and, though rooted in verifiable research and in facts, are written with the intention to leave space for imagination to enter rather than to create the illusion of a life fully recorded. 'Every life is … an inventory of objects, a pattern book of styles, in which everything can be constantly remixed and rearranged in every possible fashion'; so wrote Italo Calvino.[42] Much is left out. Austen was dead at 41: her life cut short, unfinished rather than ended—much of it unlived.

Jane Austen's life story is, even after all the biographies that have been written, in significant ways unknowable. Early on, its contours were defined by her family whose carefully culled and confected account has proved a burden for subsequent biographers: how is it possible to recognize in their official portrait of a dutiful spinster aunt the writer of such startlingly original novels—novels that, moreover, point up the constrictions of family-imposed identity? I have included no object linking her directly to romantic love, the brief period of a young woman's life that forms the central subject of her novels. Her brothers, whose fortunes were made at sea and in business or on grand landed estates, are largely omitted, in favour of female connections—her beloved sister Cassandra, her dazzling cousin Eliza de Feuillide, her dear friend Martha Lloyd, her problematic aunt Mrs Leigh Perrot. Her day-to-day adult life was lived inside a community of women.

Apart from one very particular copy of *Emma*, the famous six novels do not appear here as objects. To interpret Austen's fiction in overtly biographical terms seems wrong; it's what we do too readily with women's art. Her writings mark a moment in the history of a genre which she revolutionized. But details from the fiction are woven throughout, as befits a novelist who recorded the world around her and whose aesthetic is rooted in a materialist sensibility. In that sense, this is a writer's biography.

Other than by its inclusion among the 41, no particular object is privileged as more important; the ordering is, in the main, roughly chronological but not developmental. The reader is invited to dip in and out, without danger of losing the thread; to find in each object a different vantage point. Some of the objects are documents—written and printed texts—the usual stuff of biography. Paired with the information that visual representation brings, a dialogue opens between text and image, between reading and looking. This, then, is also an exhibition: glimpses into the life of certain objects and the life those objects disclose.

Jane Austen
A life in objects

1

Portrait of Jane Austen, *c.* 1810

Jane Austen is a tease. Her life coincided with the rise of a mass readership and a celebrity culture for the first time promoting women writers. Yet, in an age when even modest gentry families commissioned portrait miniatures and travelling painters were common, she, a writer with a growing lifetime reputation, has left no professional image.

Her female contemporaries, Mary Wollstonecraft, Catharine Macaulay, Frances Burney, Amelia Opie, Mary Shelley, Hannah More, Sarah Trimmer, all have splendid public portraits in oils, the work of professional painters, hanging in the National Portrait Gallery (NPG), London. The only image from life to capture Austen's face is this sketch made by her sister Cassandra, an averagely talented amateur. In the room where it now hangs, it is dwarfed by the grand likenesses of male Romantic poets with which it shares wall space.

Cassandra's half-length sketch shows Jane, aged about thirty-five, at the beginning of her most intense period of novel writing: portrait of the artist as a middle-aged woman, perhaps? The image is lightly executed: there is no background; the dress, arms and hands are minimally, even clumsily, drawn. The eye is attracted to the only area of detail and finish: the face. In giving it definition Cassandra has used watercolour: warm brown for the hair, pale pink for the cheeks, mixed to a darker colour to indicate shadows. She has taken pains to capture something particular in the expression. For the rest, the sketch appears unfinished. Was it abandoned out of a sense of failure or is the lack of finish part of its finished effect? The unfinished portrait drawing was a Regency fashion, as executed by professional society artists Thomas Lawrence and Richard Cosway, where the intention was to capture personality unawares, unstudied, as in life.

Austen's image expresses energy at odds with its unformed context. How do we read the unsmiling face with its compressed, downturned mouth? Is it defiant? scornful? proud? or simply guarded? What is the correspondence between a portrait and its subject? Is it a copy or an allusion? The NPG is cautious: 'This frank sketch by her sister and closest confidante Cassandra is the only reasonably certain portrait from life to show Austen's face.' In 1932 the Austen scholar R.W. Chapman, answering an enquiry from Sir Henry Hake, director of the NPG, described 'a horrid little sketch (head) by Cassandra reproduced somewhere. This cannot be of any importance.'[1]

The portrait is authentic. The product of an intimate and private connection between artist and sitter, its family provenance is water-tight. Being private, its survival is a matter of chance rather than public endorsement. Austen's niece Anna Lefroy, who lived closely with her aunt for more than twenty years, hated Cassandra's sketch, describing 'the figure' as 'hideously unlike'.[2] All portraits, but most of all private portraits, evoke conflicting emotional responses, and Anna's is an emotional not a critical response. For the audience of family and friends, each with their particular relationship and memories, the psychological space for interpretation is far narrower than for those who did not know the subject.[3] With attention focused on personal attachment it becomes hard to see the image in other terms. You and I can look at Cassandra's portrait differently, seeing something that chimes with our interpretation of Jane Austen; or for us the image can become the basis for interpretation. From here we begin to build a sense of who we think she was. This opens up a huge question: what is any portrait faithful to?

Graphite and watercolour on paper, dated *c.* 1810, the sketch is 114 × 80 mm (4½ × 3⅛ inches). Sold at Sotheby's in May 1948, part of the collection formerly owned by Charles Austen's granddaughters, it was purchased by the NPG with financial support from the Friends of the National Libraries.

Cassandra Austen
neé Leigh

Steventon 20th Augst 1775

My Dear Sister

Your Letter, for which I sincerely thank you, gave us very great pleasure, by the good account it brought of our nephew George's safe arrival at Jamaica which was a circumstance we had for many weeks been very desirous of hearing; may all your future Letters from both the young Men be as favorable in the accounts they contain of their Health & Welfare as this was. Heaven has our warmest wishes for his success at Cambridge. Many thanks for your good wishes, We are all, I thank God, in good health, and I am more nimble and active then I was last time, expect to be confined some time in November. My last Boy is very stout, and has run alone these two months, and he is not yet sixteen months old. My little Girl talks all day long, and in my opinion is a very entertaining Companion

2

Mrs Austen to Mrs Walter, 20 August 1775

Like Laurence Sterne's comical hero Tristram Shandy, immodestly beginning his personal history 'ab Ovo' ('from the egg'),[1] the infant phenomenon who became Jane Austen gave notice of her imminent arrival before assuming a place in the outside world. Her mother, Mrs Cassandra Austen, reported her latest pregnancy in this letter of 20 August 1775 to her sister-in-law Mrs Susanna Walter, the Parsonage, near Tunbridge, Kent:

> Many thanks for your good wishes, we are all, I thank God, in good health, and I am more nimble and active than I was last time, expect to be confined some time in November.[2]

Five and not six months pregnant, Mrs Austen slightly miscalculated: Jane was born on 16 December during a bitterly cold winter. The Revd George Austen, sending news of the birth the following day, wrote:

Dear Sister,

You have doubtless been for some time in expectation of hearing from Hampshire, and perhaps wondered a little we were in our old age grown such bad reckoners but so it was, for Cassey certainly expected to have been brought to bed a month ago: however last night the time came, and without a great deal of warning, everything was soon happily over. We have now another girl, a present plaything for her sister Cassy and a future companion. She is to be Jenny.[3]

When does the life of a famous person begin? With the first celebrated act or utterance? Or far earlier, because, in retrospect, much of what assumes importance was intimated long before? With death we are on more solid ground—the acclaimed deeds and great works have slotted into place. At birth everything exists in the future tense.

Jane Austen persisted in displaying a preference for beginnings: beginning her career as novelist aged eleven or thereabouts; beginning several fictions that she never got around to finishing; and, in a surprise about-turn, publishing her first novel, *Northanger Abbey*, last. Beginning a letter, she would arrange her 'important nothings' in order, thus providing a recipe for the novel of everyday life that she would invent.[4]

She was fond of announcing her novels as births: 'I can no more forget [*Sense and Sensibilty*], than a mother can forget her sucking child'; 'I have got my own darling Child [*Pride and Prejudice*] from London'; 'As I wish very much to see your Jemima, I am sure you will like to see my Emma.'[5] Actual births disgusted her.

Her nephew–biographer pompously traced the 'foundations of her fame'[6] to May 1686, almost 100 years before she was born, publishing in tedious fullness a rambling letter from that date whose utter irrelevance is compensated, in his eyes at least, by the fact it was written by Eliza Chandos, wife of the eighth Lord of Chandos and mother of the first Duke, who added to illustrious pedigree the fact that he was Handel's patron. Eliza was Jane's great-great-grandmother. The letter became a cherished family heirloom, reminding the reader of Austen's distant aristocratic origins—and, more revealingly, her family's persistent social anxiety.

Her propensity for beginnings took a speculative turn towards regeneration when in one of her letters she surmised that 'seven years I suppose are enough to change every pore of one's skin, & every feeling of one's mind.'[7] In short, she might well have agreed with Henry James (described by Rudyard Kipling as her 'one son'), who in *The Art of Fiction* observed that 'Experience is never limited, and it is never complete.'[8]

Jane Austen's great-great-nephew, Richard A. Austen-Leigh, gave Mrs Austen's letter to Jane Austen's House in October 1949—one of the museum's inaugural documents, we might say.

3

The Revd George Austen's bookcase

In the room Jane shared with her sister Cassandra as young women at Steventon Rectory, Hampshire, there stood a cheap cupboard with shelves above, painted chocolate brown, for books. Like the house, it is long gone. The rectory doubled as a boarding school, Jane's father supplementing his clerical income by coaching boys for university entrance. He had an extensive library of more than 500 volumes.[1] This handsome bookcase was his, though we do not know which titles he kept inside it. Would Jane have been permitted to open its doors and take down a volume? Perhaps; but she would have been aware that books gave her none of the opportunities that lay ahead for her brothers or her father's pupils: no admittance to university; no careers for a woman. In *Emma*, Austen's fourth novel, girls are sent to school 'to be out of the way and scramble themselves into a little education, without any danger of coming back

prodigies' (ch. 3). In *Pride and Prejudice*, Mr Bennet's library is an exclusive male preserve.

Did Jane know that of her two godmothers, both called Jane, one—Mrs Jane Musgrave, wife of her mother's cousin, the rector of Chinnor in Oxfordshire—inherited the working library of the great mathematician Sir Isaac Newton?[2] Her grandfather had bought the library from Newton's executors in 1727. Thanks to Jane Musgrave, it survived intact after her own husband's death. A godparent was a significant figure in a child's life. Jane Musgrave died when her goddaughter was twelve. It is unlikely that Jane Austen did not visit her. Did she peep inside the library?

For a woman at that time, a bookcase, like a library, would always be a bittersweet pleasure. In the riotous girls' road-trip story 'Love and Freindship', a library provokes female transgression when the enterprising Sophia uses her personal set of skeleton keys to filch banknotes from a locked drawer in a gentleman's library.[3] Jane was fourteen when she wrote this.

She was an avid lifelong reader: of novels, of course; but also of books of history, travel, politics, sermons, poetry, critical essays and magazines—almost all in borrowed copies. She lived at a time when books, especially new books, were prohibitively expensive to buy. Always a critical reader, she drives the idea of the library and of kinds of reading deep into novels, each of which implies that reader and heroine alike come to know who we are through reading; that reading matter (or its absence) is a pretty good guide to the characters of others.

On 8 February 1807, as they began a new life in Southampton, she would tease sister Cassandra, who had removed herself from all the practicalities and the upset of another domestic upheaval, warning that if she stays away she should expect, just to spite her on her return, 'Knives that will not cut, glasses that will not hold, a sofa without a seat, & a Bookcase without shelves.'[4]

But the Revd George Austen's bureau bookcase has survived with shelves intact behind its glazed doors. Dating from the 1780s, it is in the style of George Hepplewhite. Above is a moulded cornice; behind the drop front sit a series of short drawers and arched pigeonholes. Below, there are four graduated long drawers above a waved apron on outswept bracket feet. After Jane and her parents moved to Bath in 1801 on her father's retirement, the bookcase remained at the rectory, which became the home of her eldest brother James. Removed to Steventon Manor when the rectory was demolished, the bookcase was sold at auction in 1950 to the Jane Austen Society, its first major purchase. The Society gave it to Jane Austen's House, where, as is only right, it now holds books by and about her.

The beautifull Cassandra.

a novel, in twelve Chapters.

Chapter the first

Cassandra was the Daughter and the only
Daughter of a celebrated Millener in Bond Street.
Her father was of noble Birth, being the near
relation of the Dutchess of —'s Butler.

Chapter the 2d

When Cassandra had attained her 16th
year, she was lovely & amiable & chancing to
fall in love with an elegant Bonnet, her Mother
had just compleated bespoke by the Countess of
—— she placed it on her gentle Head & walked
from her Mothers shop to make her Fortune.

Chapter the 3d

The first person she met, was the Visco

4

'Volume the First'

Jane Austen's favourite word, aged twelve, was 'author'; no false ladylike modesty here. Affixed thirteen times to the overblown dedications of her capsule teenage stories by this not so 'Humble Servant', the word also intrudes, perhaps unawares, into the misspelled name of 'Sir Author' (corrected to 'Sir Arthur') in her playlet 'The Visit'. She made fair copies of sixteen short works, composed from age eleven or twelve to seventeen, into this notebook—stories, play sketches, verses and moral fragments. The final entry is dated 'June 3ᵈ 1793'. They represent some of the earliest surviving examples of her hand and art.

Written to show how clever she knew she was, these spoof tales poke fun at the limited syllabus passing for female education among well-bred families at the close of the eighteenth century. In them, she introduces young girls whose tastes run less to needlework, home economics and history lessons than to boys, gambling and strong drink. At a time when teen fiction (like the recognition of adolescence as a cultural and psychological state)

of — a young Man, no less celebrated for his Ac-
:complishments & Virtues, than for his Elegance
& Beauty. She curtseyed & walked on.

Chapter the 4th

She then proceeded to a Pastry-cooks where
she devoured six ices, refused to pay for them,
knocked down the Pastry Cook & walked away.

scarcely existed, the young Austen used wilful misreading to test
the limits of both writing and female conduct.

Her teenage characters live out appropriate teenage fantasies:
they disown their parents, run away to seek their fortunes and
invent new identities; they become orphaned only to discover
wealthy and noble relatives. Characters in flight, their adventures
lie somewhere between folk tale, fairy tale and cartoon, with their
familiar mix of economy and extraordinariness. Their stories
are prone to digression and sudden shifts in topic—devices for
postponing or altogether abandoning the ending, and for avoiding
consequence.

Nothing proceeds as you would expect in a novel by Jane Austen.
Brief sketches, they leave something unresolved. For heroines like
the foundling Eliza Harcourt Cecil and the 'beautifull' Cassandra,
the future is unprescribed, open to new possibilities. Stealing
from her foster parents and eloping with her friend's lover, Eliza
squanders a fortune, survives prison, and raises an army to destroy

her enemy, the mother of the friend she betrayed. The fake aristocrat Cassandra, daughter of a Bond Street milliner and the 'near relation' of a duchess's butler, falls in love with an elegant bonnet and rampages around London accosting and stealing from tradespeople.[2] Rebel girls, their lives spool on, frame after hectic frame, in the present continuous time of cartoon reality. No bad action goes unrewarded.

Years later, a published novelist, she shared her early notebooks with her teenage nieces and nephew in creative writing classes held at Chawton Cottage. Looking back, the writer of far different novels about circumscribed female futures, did she feel something of the longing soon to be expressed in Catherine Earnshaw's cry: 'I wish I were a girl again, half-savage and hardy, and free'?[1]

Austen's teenage voice was not heard outside the family for more than a hundred years, its members fearing exposure to public scrutiny of Aunt Jane's youthful writings. To Virginia Woolf, reading them for the first time in 1922, their content and style proved a revelation, an antidote to a popular reputation so comfortable it was oppressive.[3] After another hundred years, the antidote against Janeite cosiness that Eliza, Cassandra and their bolshie sisters administer is just as necessary. The good news is that it is just as effective.

Bound in quarter-tanned sheepskin over boards sided with common late-eighteenth-century spot-marbled paper, this quarto notebook takes its name, 'Volume the First', from the calligraphic inscription on its upper cover. Passed down in the family of Austen's youngest brother Charles, it was bought by the Friends of the Bodleian, Oxford, in 1932 for £75, considered at the time a remarkable bargain: the manuscript of another early Austen work, *Lady Susan*, selling only months later at Sotheby's, London, for £2,100.

5

Marianne Knight's dancing slippers

These dancing slippers belonged to Marianne Knight (1801–1896), the seventh child of Jane Austen's brother Edward and his wife Elizabeth. But Jane would have owned pairs just like them. In one of her absurd teenage stories, a fictional character Elizabeth Johnson recounts how she and her sister Fanny, having worn out several pairs of shoes in running across Wales, finally borrow a pair of Mama's 'blue Sattin Slippers' and, taking one each, 'hopped home from Hereford delightfully'.[1] Delicate, formal footwear for the evening and the ballroom, satin slippers would scarcely survive normal outdoor walking, never mind a route march through Wales.

Social status and fashion conspired to make gentlewomen's footwear of every sort flimsy. Dancing slippers were flimsiest of all, often disintegrating in the course of a single evening's wear. English country dances and French *contredanses* (in both of which the couples face each other in two long rows), Scottish reels, Irish jigs and hornpipes (in honour of Britain's naval victories) all involved vigorous activity. A contemporary, Susan Sibbald, recorded how she danced so hard at one ball that a hole in her slipper left her with a bleeding foot.[2]

In his brief 'Biographical Notice' of his sister, Henry Austen chose to include the detail that 'She was fond of dancing, and excelled in it.'[3] He attached the information to her posthumously published *Northanger Abbey*, a novel in which Henry Tilney, keen to educate, remarks to the heroine Catherine Morland that dancing, 'a contract of mutual agreeableness for the space of an evening' (ch. 10), is a play version of marriage.

Balls move the plot along in Austen's novels because, much like the novel itself, a dance is a codified art form and the space where relations between the sexes are tested. In *Pride and Prejudice* the dance might be private and by invitation only (Mr Bingley's ball at Netherfield Park), or a ticketed assembly held in the local town's (Meryton's) public rooms. Whatever the occasion, the dance floor measures the course of stories in which, as in *Northanger Abbey*, readers and characters 'are all hastening together to perfect felicity' (ch. 31).

Both men and women would carry their dancing slippers in bags, changing into them only on arrival at the ball. Marianne's pair does not have a left or right shoe. It was up to the owner to wear them in as suited best. Tie ribbons secured the slippers on the feet and could be crossed up the legs. The slippers' smooth leather soles would be chalked to improve their grip on polished wooden floors. At high-society balls, an artist might be commissioned to chalk the floor itself in elaborate patterns that the dancers' feet wore away over the course of the evening.

Tom Moore, poet friend of Lord Byron, describes one such dance floor chalked with the constellations:

> At every step a star is fled,
> And suns grow dim beneath their tread!
> …
> Hours are not feet, yet hours trip on,
> Time is not chalk, yet time's soon gone![4]

The dancing slipper is a token of life's fleeting joys. From their fine condition, we must assume this pair was never worn; that they never eclipsed a moon or tripped across the Milky Way. But Marianne Knight will have owned other pairs—though, since like Aunt Jane she remained unwed, none of them danced her into marriage.

Fashioned in white satin with square toes and tie ribbons, Marianne's slippers date from the early nineteenth century. The heels are lined with chamois leather and the toes with linen; the soles are pigskin. Beryl Bradford, a descendant of Edward Knight, donated them to Jane Austen's House in 1952.

6

Marriage register, St Nicholas Church, Steventon

No direct accounts survive from Jane Austen's childhood. But the parish marriage register of the church where her father was rector contains some surprising entries in her hand: marriage banns published between 'Henry Frederic Howard Fitzwilliam of London' and 'Jane Austen of Steventon'; below that, a marriage solemnized between 'Edmund Arthur William Mortimer of Liverpool' and 'Jane Austen of Steventon'; in a third entry, 'Jack Smith' and 'Jane Smith, late Austen' are witnesses to their own marriage. The insertions (with their curious anticipations of the naming of future fictional heroes) lurch from daydreams of aristocratic elevation to the commonest unions, with bigamy thrown in. This may be typical youthful autograph

The Form of an Entry of Publication of Banns.

The Banns of Marriage between *A. B.* of *London*

and *C. D.* of *Thornton*   were duly published in this

Church for the {first / second / third} Time, on Sunday the

Day of   in the Year One Thousand Seven

Hundred and

                    J. J. Rector / Vicar / Curate

The Form of an Entry of a Marriage.

A. B. of   and *C. D.* of

were married in this Church by {Banns / License*} this

Day of   in the Year One Thousand Seven

Hundred and   by me

                    J. J. Rector / Vicar / Curate

This Marriage was solemnized between us *A. B. C. B.* late *C. D.*

in the Presence of *E. F. G. H.*

* Insert these Words, viz. *with Consent of* {*Parents* / *Guardians*} where both, or either

of the Parties to be married *by License*, are under Age.

Nº 1.   Benjamin Bu[...]
both of this P[...]
married in t[...]
Eleventh Day o[...]
Lord 1755 by [...]
This Marriag[...]
Us the Mark [...]
and Hannah Bu[...]
in the Presenc[...]
Mary Edeale[...]

Nº 2.   John Brigh[...]
and Jane Li[...]
married by [...]
November i[...]
Thousand Se[...]
by Me Th[...]
This Marri[...]
the Mark resp[...]
Jane Bright[...]
in the Presen[...]
and the Mark o[...]

art, but what can have prompted defacement of an official church document— boredom, a dare, sheer naughtiness? And did her clergyman father indulge such behaviour?[1] After Lord Hardwicke's Marriage Act (1753), the marriage register was the most reliable parish record.[2]

Austen's teenage writings delight in bizarre alliances and family groupings. In a story perhaps written as early as age eleven, the lovers, Frederic and Elfrida, have names that are near-anagrams, while they themselves are identically twinned cousins. In the same story, a couple considered too young to marry are described, in another odd mirroring, as aged thirty-six and sixty-three. In 'Edgar & Emma', Sir Godfrey and Lady Marlow have at least twenty children, though no more than nine travel with them at any one time. In 'The three Sisters', Mr Watts, 'quite an old Man, about two & thirty', is unconcerned as to which sister—Fanny, Sophy or Georgiana—he marries. In 'Jack & Alice' the governess elopes with the butler, and in 'Evelyn' a gentleman, Mr Gower, marries Mrs Willis, a pub landlady.[3]

Eccentric details in early stories acquire a disturbing aspect in the adult novels where, rather than leaving them to litter the narrative surface, she sinks explosive depth charges far below. What are we to make of Colonel Brandon's love for Marianne Dashwood in *Sense and Sensibility* once we know the sensational history of the orphaned Elizas? Eliza No. 1 was Brandon's father's ward, a near relation and a girl his own age with whom he lived from earliest childhood and fell in love. Snatched from him and forcibly married to his elder brother, Eliza is divorced and abandoned to prostitution. Dying destitute, she leaves her illegitimate daughter, another Eliza, in Brandon's safe keeping. Eliza No. 2 is seduced as a teenager by Willoughby (Marianne's near-seducer), left pregnant, rescued and hidden away in the country by Brandon. Now, two Elizas down, Brandon offers himself, aged thirty-six, as the appropriate husband for seventeen-year-old Marianne, whose resemblance to the dead Elizas has long struck him (ch. 31). (Spoiler alert: Marianne does marry Brandon and finds herself immured in deepest rural Dorsetshire.) The counterfeit symmetry and antithesis that constitute the farce of her youthful writing here give way to something far more disconcerting. Austen's novels are littered with female hostages to the forces of dark romance—Georgiana Darcy, Maria Bertram, even Jane Fairfax.

The irreverent parody of the teenage writings is, like the defacing of the church register, a form of graffiti, a spontaneous and self-promoting art, written (figuratively speaking) in the margins of her favourite books: notably, the novels of Samuel Richardson, where the 'official' document of classic literature is demoted to mere support for her precocious talent. Surviving into the adult novels such defacement represents something more troubling—a blot or stain that marks the limit of Austen's mature impulse towards naturalism and the point where an alternative, anarchic reality threatens to break through.

As a young adult, Jane occasionally acted as her father's clerk, recording baptisms and deaths in the parish register.[4] The marriage register is now held at Hampshire Record Office, Winchester, on behalf of the Incumbent and Parochial Church Council of Steventon.

7

Betsy Hancock/ Eliza de Feuillide

Enter Jane Austen's muse: sophisticated socialite Eliza de Feuillide, sparkling with all the intrigue and glamour of a Georgette Heyer heroine. Here's how her story began, as plain Betsy Hancock. Betsy's mother, Philadelphia Austen, Jane's paternal aunt, having completed her apprenticeship to a Covent Garden milliner, set sail for India in January 1752 on the *Bombay Castle*. Her purpose, to hook a wealthy husband, was part of a desperate practice soon known as the fishing fleet. Arrived in Madras, Philadelphia quickly captured Tysoe Saul Hancock, an East India Company surgeon. In 1761 Hancock formed a mercantile partnership with colonial administrator Warren Hastings; Betsy was born on 22 December 1761. The Hancocks returned to England in 1765 amid rumours of a liaison between Mrs Hancock and the widowed Hastings, who had settled a trust fund of £10,000 on goddaughter Betsy. Founded or unfounded,

the rumours lingered down the years. Business soon drew Hancock back to India; he never saw wife or daughter again.

By 1779 the Hancock ladies were in Paris, where Betsy shone in society, visited Versailles and danced at a ball attended by Marie Antoinette, describing it in a letter to Phylly Walter, her English country cousin, as answering 'exactly to the description given in the Arabian Nights entertainments of enchanted palaces'.[1] Betsy was now married to a captain in the French Queen's Regiment of Dragoons, the self-styled Comte de Feuillide, though only the son of a provincial lawyer. Her transformation complete, she signed her letters to wide-eyed Phylly 'Eliza, Countess de Feuillide'.

In London in the 1780s, Eliza again inserted herself into the highest circles: a reception at St James's Palace, a party given by the Duchess of Cumberland, a ball at exclusive Almack's assembly rooms. There were amateur dramatics and flirtations with her Steventon cousins when Jane, fourteen years her junior, was smitten with her exotic relation. 'Flirtation', Eliza wrote to Phylly, 'makes the blood circulate!'[2] Trapped in England after Revolution broke out in France in July 1789, Eliza learnt at a distance of her husband's death at the guillotine. In 1797 she married Jane's brother Henry, a social animal as protean and charismatic as herself. He was ten years younger.

Once you know where to look, Eliza's influence is everywhere in Jane's life and writings: in Eliza, found as a baby in a 'Haycock' (Hancock?) in the startlingly prescient teenage story 'Henry & Eliza'; as the dedicatee of 'Love and Freindship'; in the defiant cougar Lady Susan, in the novella of that name. Eliza has regularly been linked to Austen's precocious portraits of female predators. But, viewed another way, her example, fictionally heightened, merely exposes the real limits of women's power and what they must dare to secure a future.

Though Austen's novels would transform the improbable heroines of earlier romance into English girls with English names, Betsy/Eliza, a heroine set upon a far different path, was her early inspiration. Resilient, cultured, artistic and complex, she extended cousin Jane's reading, nurtured her love of music, her knowledge of French and Italian, and encouraged her talent for writing. She opened a window onto enchanted lands: starting, perhaps, with the curries, attar of roses and scents of Arabian Nights that perfume Jane's teenage writings. In April 1811, at Henry and Eliza's fashionable Chelsea home, Austen enjoyed musical soirées, mixed with exiled French émigrés and read proofs for her first publication, *Sense and Sensibility*. She attended Eliza when she died there two years later in April 1813.

Eliza gave her portrait miniature, whereabouts now unknown, to cousin Phylly, with the inscription *Amoris et Amicitiae*—'Of Love and Friendship'. Another miniature remains in family ownership. This group portrait by Joshua Reynolds was re-identified in 2017 as Tysoe Hancock (not seen here), his wife, a young Betsy and Clarinda, the much loved family servant who accompanied them from India to London in 1765. Painted when Betsy was three and a half years old, it hung in Henry and Eliza's various London homes, where Jane Austen would have known it.[3]

8

'Juvenile Songs & Lessons': Jane Austen's music book

Despite the musicality we associate with her novels, thanks to the evocative scores of screen adaptations, Jane Austen's skill as a pianist was merely tolerated within her family. Rumour has it they slid further under the bedclothes while she pounded the keys, Mary Bennet-style, in the early mornings in the parlour below.

By 1796 at Steventon, Jane had a Ganer square piano, kept, like Mary Bennet's, in the upstairs sitting room that she shared with sister Cassandra; she was taking lessons at the time from the Winchester deputy organist and composer George Chard. But the instrument was sold when the family moved to Bath in 1801. Part of the pleasure she anticipated a few years later from a settled home at Chawton was to possess once again an instrument of her own. She writes, 28 December 1808: 'Yes, yes, we <u>will</u> have a Pianoforte, as good a one as can be got for 30 Guineas — & I will practise

My Ain Kind Dearie - with Variations by I. Corri

country dances, that we may have some amusement for our nephews & neices, when we have the pleasure of their company.'[1]

At Chawton from 1809, Jane practised every day before breakfast, her niece Caroline remembering how she played at this early hour 'when she could have the room to herself' because 'none of her family cared much for it'. But to Caroline, four years old in 1809, her aunt's playing was delightful: 'She played very pretty tunes, *I* thought—and I liked to stand by her and listen to them.'[2] Though Caroline later described her aunt's music as 'disgracefully easy', Jane was a competent performer in a private setting. She knew Haydn's music and some Mozart.

Traditional airs, popular in the period, featured largely in her repertoire. They also form part of the musical landscape of her novels: in *Pride and Prejudice* (ch. 10) Caroline Bingley plays 'a lively Scotch air', while in *Emma* (ch. 28) Jane Fairfax's piano arrives with a set of Irish melodies (in context, a reference designed to mislead), among them 'Robin Adair'. Much later, friends recalled Jane's sweet singing voice. Fulwar William Fowle, nephew of Cassandra's dead fiancé, described an 'attractive animated delightful person … I well remember her singing—& "The yellow haired Laddie" made an impression upon me, which more than half a century has had no power to efface.'[3]

This pre-ruled keyboard copybook may have been a present from Jane's cousin, Eliza de Feuillide; the first and third pieces in it are arrangements for keyboard or harp of French opera overtures copied from Eliza's own scores. Eliza was an accomplished harpist. Theirs was a musical friendship and Eliza was the source of several Continental airs. The song that Caroline described as the one she begged her aunt most often to play and sing, 'Que j'aime à voir les hirondelles', survives in a book belonging to Eliza. This album also contains several popular Scottish folk pieces: 'My Ain Kind Dearie' (pictured on previous spread), 'My Love She's but a Lassie Yet', 'Robin Gray'.

An oblong folio with full calf binding, from the firm of Longman & Broderip, No. 26 Cheapside and No. 13 Haymarket, the hand identifies it as copied by Jane Austen. It contains a repertoire of music, solo and duet, available in printed form from *c.*1790 to 1810. The title page features the publisher's engraving of a cherub holding a blank label, completed in ink with the words 'Juvenile Songs & Lessons'. Underneath is written in Jane's hand what looks like an ironic aside: 'for young beginners who don't know enough to practise'. But some of the pieces are copied from complex music that only a dedicated amateur could have played. Beryl Bradford, who gave the dancing slippers (Object 5), gifted the music book to Jane Austen's House in 1952.[4]

9
A muslin shawl

Nowhere does Jane Austen tell us her narrator is female, yet it is impossible to imagine she is not. Establishing the heroine, despite her known failings, as the reader's vantage point on the story, the narrator's complicity nurtures ours. Only in *Northanger Abbey* does a hero upset this arrangement by appearing to embody narrative voice. At twenty-four or twenty-five, Henry Tilney is more or less Austen's age at the novel's first drafting in 1799. Her least solemn hero, Henry educates the ingenuous Catherine Morland with a lightness of touch. Henry is playful and androgynous—not least in his early conversation with Catherine's chaperone Mrs Allen where he displays his intimate knowledge of muslin. 'Do you understand muslins, sir?' Mrs Allen enquires. 'Particularly well', Henry replies (ch. 3).

Muslin, originally imported from India, transformed clothing during Austen's lifetime.[1] A finely woven semi-transparent cotton, it had a variety of uses, as Henry suggests: from shawls and gowns to cravats and handkerchiefs. Though he does not venture so deep, there were weights and finishes of muslin: book muslin, cambric muslin, clear muslin, jaconet, mousseline, sprigged. Muslin was delicate—a status indicator—easily torn, as Lydia Bennet learns in *Pride and Prejudice* (ch. 47), and dirtied, its wear impractical for any below the middling or gentry ranks. Austen's letters attest to muslin's versatility—given new life by reworking into lesser items or by dyeing.[2]

Though hand-spun and hand-woven Indian muslin set the fashionable standard in the 1790s, by the late 1810s machine-made British manufacture rivalled it for price though not quality. British muslins appeared lifeless in two respects: they lacked the slight unevenness of hand-woven counterparts, as well as their perfume, absorbed from spices, such as cinnamon and cloves, packed along-side the fabric bales in cargoes for export. Of course, wily home merchants sometimes added distinctive scents to their textiles. Nevertheless, Austen makes the ability to discriminate between Indian and English a significant marker: Henry Tilney knows 'a true Indian muslin'. In the teenage tale 'Frederic & Elfrida', dedicated to Martha Lloyd 'for your late generosity to me in finishing my muslin Cloak', the Fitzroys congratulate 'the amiable Rebecca' in these enigmatic terms:

> 'Your sentiments so nobly expressed on the different excellencies of Indian & English Muslins, & the judicious preference you give the former, have excited in me an admiration of which I can alone give an adequate idea, by assuring you it is nearly equal to what I feel for myself.'[3]

By the late eighteenth century, London virtually controlled the trade of Europe, India and China. Cottons, silks, dyes, spices, perfumes, diamonds and opium were imported in vast quantities.

The India and China trades affected the lives of the Austens at first hand: on several occasions, Jane's sailor brother Frank profitably served the powerful East India Company, convoying their heavily laden ships.[4] Long before that, India was where Jane's paternal aunt made her home in 1752 and where her daughter Betsy was born. Jane may have spent much of her short life in rural Hampshire, but in reality and in imagination India exerted an abiding influence: in the sad history of Mary Wynne in the teenage story 'Kitty, or the Bower', in Lady Bertram's request for East Indian shawls in *Mansfield Park* (ch. 31) and in Martha Lloyd's recipes for curry.[5]

This Indian muslin shawl, believed to have been worked by Jane Austen, dates from the late eighteenth or early nineteenth century. Rectangular, it measures 50 × 258 cm (19¾ × 101½ inches) and was made by joining two muslin panels with a narrow border of cotton bobbin net, embroidered with satin-stitch crosses, repeating the pattern of crosses sprinkled across the fabric. The shawl is on loan to Jane Austen's House.

THE

TRIAL

OF

Mrs. LEIGH PERROT,

WIFE OF —— LEIGH PERROT, ESQ.

WHICH CAME ON AT SOMERSET ASSIZES, HOLDEN
ON THE 29TH OF MARCH, 1800, AT
TAUNTON, BEFORE

Mr. JUSTICE LAWRENCE,

ON A CHARGE OF

STEALING A CARD OF LACE:

TO WHICH ARE ADDED,

SOME CIRCUMSTANCES ATTENDANT ON THAT INTEREST-
ING TRIAL.

SECOND EDITION.

London:

Printed by J. W. Myers, No. 2, Paternoster-row,

FOR WEST AND HUGHES, NO. 40, PATERNOSTER-ROW;
AND C. CHAPPLE, NO. 66, PALL-MALL.

~~~~

1800.

10

The trial of
Mrs Leigh Perrot

Each Austen novel has its dark subplot and every family its
skeletons. Such was Jane Leigh Perrot, wife of Jane Austen's
maternal uncle. The Leigh Perrots were a wealthy couple, with
a country seat in Berkshire and a town house in Bath.

Around 1 p.m. on Thursday 8 August 1799, Mrs Leigh
Perrot called at the haberdashery shop managed by Miss
Elizabeth Gregory at No. 1 Bath Street, Bath, where she purchased a card of black lace. Later in the day the shopkeeper
approached her in the street, accusing her of stealing a card of
white lace, which was discovered on her person.

Arrested on a charge of shoplifting, Mrs Leigh Perrot was
placed in custody at Ilchester Gaol, Somerset, where she spent
seven months awaiting the next Taunton Assizes. As a gentlewoman, she was not lodged with the common prisoners but
in the house of the prison governor, Edward Scadding, joined

there by her devoted husband. Even so, her lodgings were crude enough: 'vulgarity, dirt, noise from morning till night. The people, not conscious that this can be objectionable to anybody', as she described it.[1]

The theft was a capital offence. Found guilty, she would be sentenced to hang or, more likely, to transportation for fourteen years to Botany Bay, Australia. Mrs Austen offered to send one of her daughters, Cassandra or Jane, then aged twenty-six and twenty-three, to keep their aunt company in prison. Fortunately for them, this was declined.

The trial, on 29 March 1800, in the presence of a packed courtroom, lasted seven hours. Charles Filby, the shopman laying the charge, had a shady past, while the defence rested on Mrs Leigh Perrot's social rank and testimonies to her good character as 'an example for other ladies in the parish'.[2] The jury reached a verdict of 'not guilty' in a matter of minutes. But though she was acquitted, reports published in Taunton, London and Bath, and more briefly in the provincial and national news (including two columns in *The Times* of 1 April 1800) ensured sustained exposure.[3]

Was it a sting or did she do it?[4] The evidence is far from clear. Joseph Jekyll MP, her own counsel, believed Mrs Leigh Perrot guilty; that she was a kleptomaniac. It was said, too, that her husband bought off the prosecution. On the other hand, a witness came forward to report a similar scam: that unpaid goods had been secreted into her parcel.

The Leigh Perrots continued to reside in Bath. The Austens, who moved in 1801 to that gossip-obsessed city, must have been affected by their relative's recent notoriety. Did the scandal colour Jane's persistent dislike of her aunt and her social circle, when she reported, 13 May 1801, soon after their arrival: 'Another stupid party last night; perhaps if larger they might be less intolerable'?[5] Nor did Aunt Leigh Perrot live thereafter a blameless life. Rumours circulated in 1805 that she had been caught stealing a plant from a local nursery garden.[6] If true, this time the case did not come to court.

The incident of the lace was only recorded in an authorized Austen biography in 1913.[7] But fiction has a long memory. Known for her stinginess, Mrs Leigh Perrot prompted two of her niece's meanest-spirited fictional aunts: Lady Catherine de Bourgh in *Pride and Prejudice* and Mrs Norris in *Mansfield Park*, the latter accused by her niece Maria Bertram of 'spunging' a heath plant from the gardener at Sotherton (ch. 10). More curiously, almost forty years later, the episode suggested Thomas De Quincey's melodramatic tale 'The Household Wreck', published in *Blackwood's Magazine*, January 1838.

This 32-page pamphlet is believed to be the only surviving copy of the London edition of the trial. It was gifted to Jane Austen's House in 1951 by the Austen scholar R.W. Chapman.

11

Silhouette of Cassandra Elizabeth Austen

Announcing Jane's birth, her father anticipated she would be 'a present plaything for her sister Cassy and a future companion'.[1] When Cassandra, aged twelve, was sent from home to school, Jane, aged just nine, went too, because 'if Cassandra's head had been going to be cut off Jane would have her's cut off too'.[2] In later life, they were 'the formidables', striking terror into young men's hearts.[3] When Jane died, Cassandra wrote: 'I <u>have</u> lost a treasure … She was the sun of my life.'[4]

   Though we know little of certainty about the life of Jane Austen, it is impossible to doubt the intensity of the bond with Cassandra. Theirs was a special friendship, like Vanessa Bell's with Virginia Woolf and quite unlike Charlotte Brontë's with Emily. Impossible, too, to see their relationship as other than mutually completing rather than something that brings either into sharper, individual focus.

Cassandra was her sister's primary confidante and eventually thereafter the gatekeeper of the archive. We are interested in her for the light she may shed. Their half correspondence (Cassandra's letters to Jane do not survive) now appears complexly coded because, paradoxically, the least guarded and most reliant on a shared private language. Cassandra preserved and selectively transmitted portions to the next generation, burying much out of sight, according to her niece Caroline Austen, and making it impossible to recover the whole.[5] At this distance, Cassandra can seem an occluding force.

If Jane was the sun, Cassandra was, in the words of biographer Claire Tomalin, 'the moon and shadow to Jane's brightness … never much more than a darkly seen shape';[6] or, perhaps, a silhouette. A shadow likeness seems appropriate for a shadow life. This silhouette is all we have by way of a portrait for Cassandra Austen. Popular from the second half of the eighteenth century, silhouettes were a fashionable and quick way to have one's picture made.[7] By the 1810s they were cheap enough, with professional studios appearing in spa towns and seaside resorts, and silhouettists working from booths at fairs. A silhouette portrait could be cut in a matter of minutes and taken away at once—rather like nowadays entering a photo booth at the railway station.

Ephemeral, certainly; but the silhouette had its advocates, like the physignomist Johann Caspar Lavater, who considered the profile a scientific indicator of character. His *Physiognomische Fragmente*, 1775–6, published as *Essays on Physiognomy* in English in the 1780s, included pages of silhouettes accompanied by descriptions of facial types and associated personality traits.

The silhouette connotes an absence, then, and also a distilled presence. It may have been a new fad, but in the 1790s associations with the black profile figures on classical Greek pottery gave the silhouette an aesthetic authority. To the Ancient Greeks, the shadow was identified with the soul, the human essence. Cassandra, too, is less absent than we might at first think. Her imprint is everywhere on what we know of Jane Austen's life. Silhouettes were replaced from the mid-nineteenth century by photography, described by the pioneering photographer Henry Fox Talbot as 'the art of fixing a shadow'.[8]

This oval silhouette in an ebonized and gilt metal frame is dated to the early nineteenth century. Canon Henry E. Hone, whose wife was a descendant of Jane Austen's brother Frank, gifted it to Jane Austen's House in 1956. Other silhouettes in the collection include those of Jane Austen's parents, the Revd George and Mrs Cassandra Austen; of Jane's maternal uncle and his wife, Mr and Mrs James Leigh Perrot; and of General Mathew, Governor of Grenada, and his wife Lady Jane Mathew, the parents of Jane Austen's eldest brother James's first wife.

12

A flower spray

Like the one sock that refuses to make a matching pair, not everything in life slots neatly into its
allotted place. Jane Austen's House was officially
opened to the public on Saturday 23 July 1949. In
the earliest years, only two rooms were displayed, the
rest of the House, divided into tenements after Cassandra Austen's death in 1845, carrying on its old life.
T. Edward Carpenter, who purchased the House for the
nation in 1948, soon acquired a number of letters and the
worktable at which Jane sewed. In 1940 Dorothy Darnell
had rescued the dining-room grate, and in 1949 Alberta
Burke donated a lock of Jane's hair. But with few objects
of known period or secure family provenance, notices
were placed in newspapers calling for Austen 'scraps'.[1]
Since then, the House has slowly reassumed something of
its identity of around 1810 as items of furniture, clothing,
books continue to return by gift, sale or loan.

But its unplanned life throws up puzzles and surprises that may (or may not) intrude a different time signature. In the House inventory, items CHWJA:JAH 360–364 consist of a large serving spoon, a rusty knife, a small copper alloy buckle, a rusty nail and a white clay pipe, all found under the floorboards. Found objects might with equal accuracy be labelled lost. Where and to whom did they belong? Once useful, they have become debris, but discovered inside a literary house or other historic site they must be meticulously recorded and conserved. Diverted from the rubbish dump and catalogued, they assume low-grade aestheticization. Like the detail that refuses to explain itself, they just might matter.

Take this spray of artificial flowers, found in 1978 in the rafters of an outbuilding and held inside a Roger & Gallet Jean Marie Farina soapbox. Faded in colour, some of the flowers threaded together with beads to form small chains, the spray has been dated to *c.* 1800. It is an evocative object, but of what? From Bath, 2 June 1799, Jane wrote to Cassandra, who had commissioned her to search for hat decorations:

> Flowers are very much worn, & Fruit is still more the thing.— Eliz: has a bunch of Strawberries, & I have seen Grapes, Cherries, Plumbs & Apricots … A plumb or green gage would cost three shillings;—Cherries & Grapes about 5 I beleive—but this is at some of the dearest Shops;—My Aunt has told me of a very cheap one near Walcot Church, to which I shall go in quest of something for You.[2]

A week later, 11 June, she reported: 'We have been to the cheap Shop, & very cheap we found it, but there are only flowers made there, no fruit … I cannot help thinking that it is more natural to have flowers grow out of the head than fruit.—What do you think on that subject?' Resolving the dilemma of fruit or flowers towards the end of the same letter, she points out that, having overspent on a black lace veil, a joint present, she finds, after all, 'it is my duty to economise for you in the flowers'.[3]

Produced from the rafters as if by magic, the flower spray lacks the provenance of items passed down within the family, inscribed in Austen's hand or bought at auction. It is as elusive as the elliptical and contingent details of her Bath letters. In both, meaning remains local, unattached to a larger life. More effectively than the securely labelled item, such detail reminds us of the essential nature of curiosity, which is, after all, a distributed condition, belonging both to the observer and to the object observed—make of it what we will.

13

Frances Burney, *Camilla*, 1796

As far as we know, Jane Austen's name appeared in print only twice in her lifetime: as 'Miss J. Austen, Steventon' in the subscription list inside Frances Burney's *Camilla* (1796), and as 'Miss Jane Austen', alongside 'Mr and Mrs Edward Austen of Godmersham' in *Two Sermons* (1808) by the Revd T. Jefferson of Tunbridge.[1] Further instances may come to light, but subscription was falling out of favour. It was, too, an expensive show of support from a woman of limited means when new publications were luxury items. This is implied in her explanation for underwriting Jefferson's work: 'I have now some money to spare … how right & how gratifying such a measure w^d be.'[2] But twelve years earlier *Camilla* represented something different.

By 1796 she knew herself to be a novelist, with drafts of 'Elinor and Marianne' and 'First Impressions' in preparation. As subscriber, her name circulated in print not only in appreciative

Mr. Andrews, Worcefter, 4 fets
J. J. Angerftein
Mrs. Angerftein
Mifs Angerftein
George Anguifh, Prebendary of Norwich
Mrs. Anfon
Robert Arbuthnot, Efq. Secretary to the Board
   of Truftees, Scotland
Mifs E. Arbuthnot
George Auft, Efq.
Mifs J. Auften, Steventon
Mrs. Ayton

B

His Grace the Duke of Beaufort, K. G.
Her Grace the Duchefs of Beaufort
Her Grace the Duchefs Dowager of Beaufort
Her Grace the Duchefs of Buccleugh
The Marquis of Blandford
Countefs Dowager Bathurft
Earl of Beverley
Countefs of Beverley
Countefs of Befborough, 2 fets
Countefs of Bellamont
Vifcountefs Bandon
Rt. Hon. Lady Bruce
Rt. Hon. Lady Bridget Bouverie
Hon. W. H. Bouverie
Hon. Mrs. Brudenel
Rt. Hon. Edmund Burke, 5 fets

Hon.

Hon. Mrs. Bofcawen,
Hon. Mrs. Barrington
Hon. Mrs. Bethel
Sir Charles Roufe Bo
Lady Beaumont
Sir Charles Bunbury,
Lady Burrel
Lady Hunter Blair
Sir Jofeph Banks, K.
Lady Banks
Lady Crawley Boevey
Lady Smith Burges
Sir Charles Blagden
Edward Baber, Efq.
Mr. Bailey
Mrs. Baker, Salt-Offi
Mrs. Baker
Mrs. Baker
Mrs. Baldwin
Mrs. Banks
Mifs Banks
J. Cleaver Banks, Efc
Thomas Baratt, Efq.
Rev. Mr. Barbauld
Mrs. Barclay
Mrs. Barnard
John Barnes, Efq.
Mrs. Bateman
J. T. Batt, Efq.
Mrs. Batt
James Beattie, LL. D

association with that of 'F. d'Arblay' (as Burney signed herself in her 'Dedication') and 'The Author of *Evelina* and *Cecilia*' (so styled on the title page) but in the same list as 'Miss Edgeworth' and 'Mrs Hannah More'—three of the most celebrated women writers of the age. In their company, Austen's subscription, at a cost of one guinea, looks less like patronage and more like a secret pledge to the career she saw unfolding before her.[3] It anticipated, too, the letter her father would soon write to Thomas Cadell, publisher of *Camilla*, offering 'a manuscript novel … about the length of Miss Burney's "Evelina"'.[4]

The French essayist Roland Barthes called it *l'autonymie* (autonymy) when a barber gets a haircut, a cook makes herself dinner or a writer reads a book—something that reproduces and reverses, a dislocation of what we understand.[5] In adult Austen's case, autonymy is extreme: she only ever acknowledges herself a reader—her name inscribed in ink in others' books, never in life printed inside her own.

Allusions to *Camilla* are woven into *Northanger Abbey* and *Sanditon*. In the former, *Camilla* represents what is great in the modern female-written novel (ch. 5)—a view that the boorish John Thorpe helpfully enforces by considering it 'the horridest nonsense' (ch. 7). In *Sanditon* Charlotte Heywood takes up *Camilla* as she lingers in Mrs Whitby's library musing on the intersections between fiction and reality (ch. 6). Subscription and less exclusive circulating libraries infiltrate Austen's novels. Exiled from Mansfield Park, Fanny Price finds consolation and some independence in subscribing to the Portsmouth library (ch. 40). In *Pride and Prejudice*, soldier-mad Lydia Bennet discovers new enthusiasm for books on learning that Colonel

Forster and Captain Carter are 'very often standing in Clarke's library' (ch. 7).

The lending library was a regular marker of civic elegance. According to one popular guidebook, 'the taste and character of individuals may be better learned in a library than in a ball-room.'[6] Is this why Dawlish is made the home town of vulgar Lucy Steele in *Sense and Sensibility*? A pointed reference to Dawlish in a letter of 1814 recalls a visit there in 1802 and a 'particularly pitiful & wretched' library, 'not likely to have anybody's publication'.[7] By 1814 Austen's own novels were in library circulation.

Libraries provided the bulk of her reading matter: in 1798 she subscribed to Mrs Martin's Basingstoke library; from 1809 she had the Alton Book Society, declared superior to its rival at nearby Steventon and Manydown.[8] Book societies defrayed high costs by sharing volumes and allocating reading to timed slots. In her last years and in London, her publisher John Murray loaned new books from his list—a glamorous kind of borrowing.[9]

Date unknown, reading *Camilla* became writing *Camilla*. Pencilled words enveloping the printed 'FINIS' in volume 5 of Jane Austen's copy, now in the Bodleian Library, Oxford, suggest a reader's revenge upon Dr Marchmont, whose sceptical opinion of women delays the heroine's happiness. Unfortunately, the insertion was cropped during rebinding; we will never know the fate Austen prescribed for him—death or, worse still, marriage?[10]

Paragon – Tuesday May 2.

My dear Cassandra.

For your letter from Kintbury & for all
the compliments on my writing which it contained I now
return you my best thanks. — I am very glad that Martha
goes to Chilton; a very essential temporary comfort her
presence must afford to Mrs Craven, and I hope she
will endeavour to make it a lasting one by exerting
those kind offices in favour of the young Man, from
which you were both with-held in the case of the
Harrison family by the mistaken tenderness of one
part of ours. — The Endymion came into Portsmouth
on Sunday, & I have sent Charles a short letter by
this days post. — My adventures since I wrote to
you three days ago have been such as the time would
easily contain; I walked yesterday morning with
Mrs Chamberlayne to Lyncombe & Widcombe, and
in the evening I drank tea with the Holders. Mrs
Chamberlayne's pace was not quite so magnificent
on this second trial as in the first; it was nothing
more than I could keep up with, without effort; &
for many, many yards together on a raised narrow
footpath I led the way. — The walk was very beautif

14

A letter, 26–27 May 1801

A promise lies tucked inside a letter, nestling there like a secret; and writers thrive on secrets. Jane Austen wrote this letter, dated 26–27 May 1801, aged twenty-five, over two days from Bath to her sister Cassandra, on a visit to family friends in Berkshire. Jane and her parents had been in Bath only a few weeks; they were house hunting. She describes one property where the kitchen is damp and another with a gloomy aspect. 'I have nothing more to say on the subject of Houses', she adds wearily.[1] Intriguing references to a Mr Evelyn and his 'very bewitching Phaeton' make us wish to know more: how far did she encourage the flirtation she hints at between them? and how did he acquire his reputation for danger? Did he use his flashy carriage, like John Thorpe in *Northanger Abbey* (ch. 11), to seduce young women or was he really only driving into the countryside (unlikely as it sounds) to collect birdseed?

A postscript written, for economy's sake, upside down between the lines of page 1 includes news of brother Charles, a junior naval officer. With his share of prize money from the capture of an enemy ship he has bought his sisters 'Gold chains & Topaze Crosses'. Outside London, with its own postal service, postage—based on weight and distance travelled—was paid by the recipient. This acted as an incentive for the writer to fill every scrap of paper.

Jane Austen invented a new voice for fiction: conversational and intimate. Though early experiments in the novel were written as fictional letters, her novels are the first to see in the domestic letter, filled with what she describes as 'little matters',[2] a future for the novel as a study of life's everyday events. Her letters are the shadow life of her novels. Topics tumble over one another in a freewheeling stream of views and gossip. The voice appears artless. But, unpacked, letters, much like her chattering spinster Miss Bates from *Emma*, another 'great talker upon little matters' (ch. 3), yield far more than at first appears.

In her letters, and nowhere else, Austen speaks in her own voice. But that voice is mediated and performative, attuned to its implied reader. She must have written several thousand: as a dependent female in a large and dispersed family, this was one of her sociable duties. Women for centuries took on this task. Cassandra was her chief correspondent. Some time before her death in 1845, Cassandra distributed those letters she had kept as mementoes among surviving family members. This letter descended to Charles Austen and thence to his granddaughters, who, hard up, sold it in the 1920s, part of a larger cache of relics and manuscripts. It was accompanied in its wanderings by the gold chains and topaz crosses that Jane here reports Charles has bought for them. Years later, his gift provided the idea for the 'very pretty amber cross' that William Price, a young sailor modelled on Charles, brought from Sicily for his sister Fanny in *Mansfield Park* (ch. 26).

Her letters are the key to everything: raw data for her life and the untransformed banalities which, magically transmuted, become the precious trivia of the novels. Occasionally, as here, they read like the preliminary jottings of a fiction-making mind—the artfulness of the talking voice that runs on.

American Austen enthusiast Charles Beecher Hogan purchased letter and crosses in November 1926. He later gave the crosses as a wedding present to his wife. In 1974 Hogan presented letter and crosses to the Jane Austen Society.[3] Since 2020 they have formed part of the Jane Austen's House collection.

15

Portrait of Jane Austen, 1804

Each portrait is a kind of truth, and every portrait is a lie—or so it goes. Two amateur sketches of Jane Austen by her sister Cassandra have come down to us. One, made *c.* 1810, is now in the National Portrait Gallery, London (see Object 1); the other, executed six years earlier, remains in family ownership. This portrait in pen and ink and watercolour is dated and signed with Cassandra's initials 'CEA 1804'; the 1810 sketch is unsigned. Neither portrait names the sitter; for that we rely on family attribution.

Jane Austen's name gives both portraits credibility and purpose even as we question whether they look like her. And that question looms particularly large in this 1804 watercolour. Jane is sitting out of doors, by a tree, perhaps on a bank, from which she surveys her surroundings. But, apart from the glimpse of a curved pink cheek, there is no face

to this back-view portrait;[1] so, too, the setting is a vacant blank. The viewer's eye is drawn, with the sitter's, into emptiness. There is detail and colour: dress and poke bonnet throw the emphasis on costume. Cassandra has liberally employed the indigo, Prussian blue and lampblack in her paintbox. In fact, it has been commented that she may have based this earlier sketch upon a popular fashion plate.[2]

In some ways this portrait is more finished than Cassandra's later attempt. Though it withholds the very information we expect a portrait to give—what does she look like and where is she—in the immediate family it met with approval as an image of Aunt Jane, her niece, Anna Lefroy, writing in 1862: 'I would give a good deal, that is as much as I could afford, for a sketch which Aunt Cassandra made of her in one of their expeditions—sitting down out of doors, on a hot day, with her bonnet strings untied.'[3] What might fill the empty prospect? In 1804 the Austens spent the summer by the sea, in Devon and Lyme Regis on the Dorset coast. Is Jane looking out to sea? There were family rumours of a holiday romance.

After Cassandra's death in 1845, both portraits became the property of another niece, another Cassandra (known as Cassy Esten), the daughter of Charles, the youngest Austen sibling. At some point in the 1860s Cassy offered Anna Lefroy her choice between the two, and she promptly took this back view, explaining that the 'Figure' in the 1810 portrait was 'so hideously unlike'; while in the back view 'the Figure only is attempted, and in that there is a good deal of resemblance'.[4]

Anna's comments establish the presence and assumed authenticity of both sketches in family conversation mid-century. She assesses their likeness to someone intimately known but now a distant memory. But what does she mean by 'the Figure being so hideously unlike' in the one sketch, and 'the Figure only is attempted' in the other? I don't think she is worried by clumsy execution or the lightly drawn contours of the overall compositions. The *Oxford English Dictionary* helps here. Among its definitions of 'figure' it gives: 'appearance, attitude, posture' (1c). In other words, the term encompasses something more than body shape. What Anna seems to be saying is that, with less attempted in the 1804 back view, more is achieved by way of likeness; that she recognizes something characteristic in the way the sitter holds herself—alert, absorbed, her left hand upon her knee. Did Cassandra capture a familiar and since remembered pose?

If she had lived into old age, there might have been a daguerreotype of Jane Austen, as there is of her brother Admiral Sir Francis Austen. And that too would be contentious.

16

Wallpaper fragment

Looking back from the 1850s to her childhood sixty years before, Anna Lefroy recalled the two rooms, bedroom and dressing room, shared by her aunts Cassandra and Jane as young women at Steventon Rectory in the 1790s. She remembered 'the common-looking carpet with its chocolate ground ... A painted press, with shelves above for books ... my Aunt Jane's Pianoforte ... scanty furniture and cheaply papered walls.'[1] Around 1800, wallpaper was a relatively recent innovation in modest gentry homes, which, as Austen's nephew–biographer James Edward Austen-Leigh noted, contained few luxuries. The Revd Austen's account with a local Basingstoke furnishers tells us that the Steventon wallpaper was blue.[2]

In 1807 Thomas Hope published a pattern book, *Household Furniture and Interior Decoration*, credited, by the *Oxford English Dictionary*, with the first English usage of the term 'interior decoration', to denote 'the planned co-ordination for artistic effect of colours and furniture, etc., in a room or building'. The thoroughness of Hope's high-end designs for his well-heeled clients ranged

from coordinated sofas and upholstery to vases and tableware. The period saw an explosion in consumerism that trickled down to middle-class families who, aping the rich, were drawn into projects for domestic makeovers and displays of good taste—then, as now, an anxious business.

Around the same time, interiority took on some of its familiar psychological associations of inwardness and privacy. As one critic has put it, 'The interior furniture of houses appeared together with the interior furniture of minds.'[3] Where Hope, Josiah Wedgwood and others perfected, through colour, form and fabric, domestic space as a private theatre for self-expression, Jane Austen is one of the earliest novelists for whom domestic space mirrors the inner life of the heroine. She deals, as Virginia Woolf might have said of her, 'with the feelings of women in a drawing-room', where 'the very walls are permeated by their creative force'.[4] With Austen's domestically confined heroine the complex life of the mind takes centre stage.

Much as the design of this leaf-patterned wallpaper brings the outdoors inside, transforming a dining room into an elegant green arbour, Austen makes architectural and psychological, objective and subjective, aspects of interiority reinforce one another. She regularly conjures felt life from material things: in her letters, tables and pianos talk and send their love;[5] in *Mansfield Park* (ch. 46) the squalor of her Portsmouth home, with 'the tea-board never thoroughly cleaned, the cups and saucers wiped in streaks, the milk a mixture of motes floating in thin blue', pulls a nauseated Fanny Price back into an object world whose physical properties reflect her psychological dissociation.

This wallpaper fragment was discovered in 2018 behind a cupboard in the dining room of Chawton Cottage. A partial tax stamp on the back helps date it: wallpaper was taxed in England from 1712 until 1836. Patterned in vibrant green leaves, possibly inspired by a type of dead nettle, it is edged by a flocked border, showing a dark green vine on a yellow background. The paper is dirty and faded, but a small area, hidden beneath the border, reveals bright 'arsenic' green—a colour popular in the early nineteenth century.

In 1809, before his mother and sisters moved in, Jane's brother Edward Knight undertook various improvements to the cottage. The walls may have been papered then. If so, did its pattern recall for Jane the leafy shade of Kitty's Bower, where the heroine of her teenage story withdrew to read and daydream?[6] The design, now known as 'Chawton Leaf', was reproduced by historic specialists Hamilton Weston Wallpapers and printed using the traditional hand-blocking technique. It again hangs in the dining room.

17

Martha Lloyd's Household Book

'I am very fond of experimental housekeeping', Jane wrote to her sister Cassandra in November 1798.[1] This recipe book was in use at Chawton Cottage during Jane Austen's lifetime. It belonged to Martha Lloyd, a close friend, ten years older than Jane, living with the Austen women. Many household duties devolved to Martha. Into her book she transcribed recipes from friends and family, much as Harriet Smith gathers riddles in *Emma* (ch. 9). 'A receipt for a Pudding' to tempt the vicar is written in verse and attributed to Jane's mother, who was known for her humorous poems. The earliest entries can be dated to the 1790s and the latest to 1830, by which time Martha was the second wife of Jane's brother Frank.

Although printed cookery books were available in the eighteenth century, handwritten collections of family recipes remained common well into the twentieth, as repositories for all sorts of domestic lore: dishes to cook; herbal remedies both efficacious and superstitious, like Martha's 'Remedy for the Hooping Cough'; and tips for cleaning ('To whiten Silk Stockings'). Several favourite dishes noted in Austen's letters—'A Harrico of Mutton', 'Toasted Cheese', 'Pickled Cucumbers' and apple puddings—feature in Martha's collection.[2]

At Chawton Cottage visitors can still see hanging from the bakehouse rafters the hoisting winch (surviving from when the cottage was a farmhouse) where pigs were jointed for the table. Martha's book contains six recipes for curing, pickling and preparing pork. The Austen women employed a cook, whose skill Jane described in 1811 as 'at least tolerable;—her pastry is the only deficiency'.[3] Cassandra kept bees; Mrs Austen grew potatoes; and the garden held apricot, apple and plum trees as well as rhubarb, raspberry canes, gooseberry and currant bushes.

If Martha's book is anything to go by, much of the garden fruit became wine: mead, currant, elderberry and gooseberry wine. Then there were emergency supplies of 'Ginger Beer fit to drink in 24 hours'. There is no recipe for Martha's favourite spruce beer; even its modern-day official website cannot summon up more enthusiasm than to describe it as cola with cheeky notes of disinfectant. For preference, though, Jane's tipple was French wine, the best incentive for a visit to brother Edward at Godmersham Park, where, on 1 July 1808, amid 'Elegance & Ease & Luxury', she anticipates 'I shall eat Ice & drink French wine.'[4]

The heroines of her teenage mini-novels are a boozy lot, not to be messed with when they've had one too many: like the bad-tempered drunk Alice Johnson, 'a little addicted to the Bottle & the Dice' in 'Jack & Alice'.[5] Perhaps coincidentally, Jane used the same style of quarto-format shop-bought notebook as Martha's to copy out her teenage fictions, many of which mock good housekeeping as a cornerstone of female education. In several early stories food and books are equally abused, the failure to follow recipes providing the engine of her rebellious comedy. In 'Lesley-Castle', written when she was aged sixteen, the inopportune death of the bridegroom leaves Charlotte Luterell with a massive wedding feast to consume and no guests to eat it. The situation calls for a 'Devouring Plan'![6] Policing women's relationship to food and fiction—the accusation of bingeing upon both—has a long and vexed history; already as a child Austen grasped this.

Martha's book shows signs of heavy domestic use. Many of its leaves have water, oil or cooking stains. Martha Lloyd's name appears on the inside of the back cover. T. Edward Carpenter, who restored Chawton Cottage in the late 1940s as Jane Austen's House, purchased Martha's household book in 1956 from Rosemary Mowll, a descendant of Jane's brother Frank. Its price was £5. He bequeathed it to the museum on his death in 1969.[7]

18

Austen family quilt

Strenuously denying Austen's writing life, early family biographers diverted attention towards her domestic employments. She was 'fond of work', 'spent much time in writing', recorded Caroline Austen, a child witness to Aunt Jane's daily routine. 'Work' turns out to be sewing shirts; 'writing' is letters.[1] Occupations approved for gentry women were in economic terms false: painting in watercolours, playing the piano, the fiddly filigree work of pinning and gluing paper scrolls embraced by the too obliging Steele sisters in *Sense and Sensibility* (ch. 23). False, because, though turning the day's tedium to some use, they did not make women economically productive—no money was earned and no value exchanged. We are all familiar with the discounted nature of much female labour.

Not until *Sanditon*, the novel left unfinished at her death, does making wealth figure overtly in the commercial speculators Mr Parker and Lady Denham. Normally, Austen occludes society's economic base, so crucial to her fictions, by confounding it with domestic happiness inside a feminized environment. Call this the

quilt-maker's perspective. On occasion, it draws in male activities, as in Captain Harville's contrivances for 'domestic happiness' in *Persuasion*: 'He drew, he varnished, he carpentered, he glued' (ch. 11).

We cannot doubt that Austen published to make money. She sold her first manuscript, a version of *Northanger Abbey*, in 1803 at the precise moment when her father's retirement and her own rejection of a marriage offer signalled a decline in her material prospects. Profits from fiction might afford some financial security. Where the novel genre developed by encoding the difference between male and female spheres, the form's preoccupation with happiness as material satisfaction can be read as a kind of distributive justice, especially in the hands of female earners. It is no coincidence that at a time when women writers were entering the marketplace in increasing numbers, their works regularly cross-referenced each other's titles—female solidarity, you might say.

What of this quilt? Inside her confected Victorian biography, the cosy myth of Aunt Jane's domestic pastimes masks her productivity as working author. But sewing, like letter writing, is not redundant work; it is necessary to social functioning. Unpicked and viewed in another light, the quilt's work processes deny the effacement they were intended to promote. Like the quilt-maker's, Austen's novelistic art is fashioned from the fabric of life's bits and pieces. Both explore connections within a female culture of repetition and recycling that sees no dichotomy between needle and pen. On 31 May 1811 Jane wrote to Cassandra, staying with brother Edward, 'Have you remembered to collect peices for the Patchwork?—We are now at a stand still.'[2] Godmersham needles were always busy making clothes for Edward's eleven children, and scraps would be left over. In a late letter she described her interlocking narrative style as twigs woven into a nest,[3] while in a surprising acknowledgement the young Samuel Beckett wrote in 1935 of his admiration for 'Jane's manner', defining it as 'material that can be treated most conveniently in the crochet mode'.[4]

The female household at Chawton made this linen and cotton patchwork coverlet, measuring approximately 262 × 232 cm (103 × 91¼ inches), around 1810. Its diamond-shaped central motif features a design of birds and a basket of flowers. A panel of 249 smaller diamonds surrounds this, each bordered by separate black and white polka-dot print strips. The outer edge is formed of over 2,500 tiny diamonds. Symmetrical and intricate, it is composed of at least 64 fabrics and uses the English paper-piecing method: fabric attached to paper shapes, hand-stitched together, the paper then removed.[5] In 1950 the quilt was among the earliest family loans to Jane Austen's House, made by Mrs Christopher Knight. On her death, it was bequeathed to the Jane Austen Society, who gifted it to the House in 2020.

19

Jane Austen's writing table

I might have chosen her portable writing box, a gift in 1794 from her father and almost lost forever when a carriage, hurtling towards Gravesend, parted her from it. She described the incident to Cassandra, 24 October 1798: 'After we had been here a quarter of an hour it was discovered that my writing and dressing boxes had been by accident put into a chaise ... driven away towards Gravesend in their way to the West Indies.'[1] The box, with its drawers and hidden spaces, contained 'Treasures' which she permitted little Catherine Foote to examine one wet Sunday morning in February 1807.[2] Joan Austen-Leigh, Austen's great-great-great-niece, gifted it in 1999 to the British Library, London, where it is on permanent display. Its contents included eyeglasses said to be Austen's (though that's unlikely), an ink pot and pen knife.

In his 1958 study, published in English as *The Poetics of Space*, the French philosopher Gaston Bachelard considered our emotional responses to built spaces—attics, cellars, drawers—any objects with deep recesses which might function as memory chests and what he called the 'veritable organs of the secret psychological life'. 'Every poet of furniture', he wrote, 'knows that the inner space of an old wardrobe is deep.'[3] So, too, the inner spaces of a writing box. But what of the power of a simple table top?

Family tradition tells us that Jane Austen set her box (pictured opposite) upon this small, twelve-sided walnut tripod table, placed by a window for light in the family room at Chawton Cottage. The table knew the pressure of her resting elbow as she pondered phrase or word, or stared out of the window searching for inspiration. Why choose such a tiny table: only 47 cms (18½ inches) in diameter? She was a neat, tidy worker, her writing disciplined and unencumbered. The table's small surface, like the small home-made booklets into which she wrote, may have reinforced the restraint that character-ized her style of composition: no room here for scattered leaves, or piles of notes in draft; certainly no space for a tea cup and the threat its liquid contents would pose to inked paper. In her novels, women must learn the art of living exposed and within limited bounds. On the table everything is laid bare. Where the writing box's recesses, its drawers and lock, invite romantic absorption, a metaphor for the unseen workings of creativity, the table asks us to contemplate the everyday materials of construction—physical placement rather than psychological displacement. It poses a harder question too: how is it even possible to find the imagination in the materials we all share—a table, pen, ink and paper?

Some time in the nineteenth century the table passed to an Austen family servant, William Littleworth.[4] The Knight family, descendants of Jane's brother Edward, bought back the table in 1913. On the underside a note reads:

This table was bought by Montagu Knight of Chawton House from a grandson of James Goodchild, who lived in Chawton village in Jane Austen's time. His brother-in-law, William Littleworth, was footman to Mrs George Austen, Jane's mother and when he was too old for work she furnished a cottage near the pond for him. Amongst the furniture was this table at which Littleworth often saw Jane Austen writing. Only the top is original.

The top dates from the early eighteenth century, while the base may be seventeenth century. Long displayed at Jane Austen's House, the table was donated to the Jane Austen Society by Brigadier B.C. Bradford, Montagu Knight's great-nephew, in late 1957 or early 1958, and in 2020 gifted by the Society to Jane Austen's House.

20

Four Wedgwood serving dishes

Jane Austen liked shopping. On trips to London she quartered the area between Covent Garden, fashionable Mayfair and as far as Marylebone with steely determination. She bought poplin at Layton & Shear's, 11 Henrietta Street, next door to brother Henry's bank; gloves at Remnant's, 126 The Strand; linen at Christian & Son, 11 Wigmore Street, and at Newton's in Leicester Square; fabrics at Flint's (Grafton House), Soho. A dinner service was inspected at Wedgwood's showrooms, 8 St James's Square, south of Bond Street. Hatchard's, London's oldest bookshop at 187 Piccadilly, and Lock & Co., hatters of St James's, still stand where they did, as does the grocer's Fortnum & Mason, which opened on Piccadilly in 1707. Her letters are filled with the small but exquisite triumphs of purchases run to ground.

Sense and Sensibility is the only novel, after the rampages of the teenage writings, in which the reader accompanies Austen's heroines around London. There is even the curious sense from her three London letters, written while she proofread the novel there in April 1811, that Austen's footsteps are forever crossing those of the Dashwood sisters as they pursue their errands.

Lying between leisure and a form of work, shopping gave gentry women a legitimate sphere of public agency.[1] It was now that 'just looking' became respectable. Going shopping is one of the few purposive activities structuring women's lives in all her novels: the walk most days to a Meryton milliner's shop in *Pride and Prejudice* (ch. 7); Molland's, a fashionable confectioner's in Milsom Street, Bath, site of a charged encounter between Anne Elliot and Captain Wentworth in *Persuasion* (ch. 19). Shopping shapes the female day and therefore the Austenian plot. It provides opportunity to form critical opinions: in the Dashwood sisters' observation of an as yet unknown Robert Ferrars lingering over a toothpick case at Gray's on Sackville Street in *Sense and Sensibility* (ch. 33). In the scene set at Ford's, 'the shop first in size and fashion' in Highbury, Emma Woodhouse, standing quietly amused in the doorway, has an epiphany, the narrator commenting, 'A mind lively and at ease, can do with seeing nothing, and can see nothing that does not answer' (ch. 27). In this moment, in a shop doorway, a manifesto for a new kind of fiction is proclaimed: the novel of women's ordinary lives.

On 6 June 1811 Austen wrote from Chawton to Cassandra:

On Monday I had the pleasure of receiving, unpacking & approving our Wedgwood ware. It all came very safely, & upon the whole is a good match, tho' I think they might have allowed us rather larger leaves, especially in such a Year of fine foliage as this. One is apt to suppose that the Woods about Birmingham must be blighted. — There was no Bill with the Goods — but that shall not screen them from being paid. I mean to ask Martha to settle the account. It will be quite in her way, for she is just now sending my Mother a Breakfast set, from the same place.[2]

These four quarter-circle-shaped Wedgwood serving dishes with oak-leaf pattern are similar to those from the Austens' set that, as the letter suggests, was added to over time. Josiah Wedgwood, from an established family of Staffordshire potters, made fine table-ware. He counted among his customers George III's wife, Queen Charlotte, and, in *Northanger Abbey*, Austen's General Tilney, who 'thought it right to encourage the manufacture of his country; and for his part, to his uncritical palate, the tea was as well flavoured from the clay of Staffordshire, as from that of Dresden or Sêve' (ch. 22). These dishes were a gift to Jane Austen's House in 2018 from a member of the Jane Austen Society of North America.

21

Theatre bill for
The Clandestine Marriage,
Covent Garden, 1813

On rare occasions we can satisfy a very particular curiosity and pinpoint Jane Austen's exact location at a precise time on a given day—call it respectful stalking. Writing to sister Cassandra from 10 Henrietta Street, London, brother Henry's home, on Wednesday 15 September 1813, she announced a trip to the theatre in prospect for that evening: 'Fanny & the two little girls are gone to take Places for to-night at Covent Garden; Clandestine Marriage & Midas'.[1] She was on a jaunt to London with brother Edward and three of his daughters: Fanny, Lizzie and Marianne. During the day, she was shopping, visiting her dressmaker, having her hair done.

This is a playbill for the performance Austen's party attended. She loved the theatre, taking in plays of all kinds whenever the

THEATRE ROYAL, COVENT-GARDEN

This prefent WEDNESDAY, Sept 15, 1813,

Will be acted the Comedy of The

Clandeftine Marriage.

Lord Ogleby by Mr. TERRY,
(Being his fecond appearance at this Theatre.)
Sir John Melvil by Mr. BARRYMORE,
Sterling by Mr BLANCHARD,
Lovewell by Mr. ABBOTT, Canton by Mr. FARLEY
Brufh by Mr HAMERTON, Sergeant Flower Mr CRESWELL
Traverfe Mr Brook, Trueman Mr Atkins, John Mr Crumpton
Mrs. Heidelberg by Mrs. DAVENPORT,
Mifs Sterling by Mrs GIBBS,
Fanny by Mifs COOKE,
Betty by Mrs KENNEDY,
(Being her fecond appearance on this ftage)
Chambermaid, Mifs TREBY, Trufty, Mrs COATES.

To which will be added *(fecond time this feafon)* the Burletta of

M I D A S.

The Overture Compofed by Mr. BISHOP.
The new Scenery painted by Meff. Whitmore, Pugh, Grieve, & their affiftants.

IMMORTALS.

Jupiter, Mr. TINNEY, Apollo, Mr. SINCLAIR, Pan, Mr. EMERY.
Mars, Mr. HIGMAN, Bacchus, Mr. DURUSET, Mercury, Mr. HEATH.
Vulcan, Mr. NORRIS, Ganymede, Mr. YARNOLD, Cupid, Mafter WILSON,
Juno, Mifs LOGAN, Minerva, Mrs DAVIES, Venus, Mifs TREBY, Iris, Mrs FINDLAY
The Graces, Mifs Standen, Mrs Heath, Mifs H. Bologna.

MORTALS.

Midas, Mr. LISTON, Sileno, Mr. TAYLOR,
Damætas, Mr. BROADHURST, Shepherd, Mr. HOWELL,
Countrymen, Meff. Everard, Lee, Linton, Little, Montague, J.Taylor, Terry, Tett, S. Tett, Williams
Lads, Meff. Brown, Grant, Louis, Platt, Powers, Sarjant, Yarnold
Myfis, Mrs LISTON, Daphne, Mrs STERLING,
Nyfa by Mifs RENNELL,
Laffes, Mefds. Adami, Bologna, Carew, Coates, Cox, Grimaldi, Herbert, Hibbert, Iliff, Louis,
Ryall, Watts, Whitmore.

A Private Box may be had nightly, on application to Mr. Brandon at the Box-office.
Boxes 7s. Second Price 3s 6d.—Pit 3s 6d. Second Price 2s.
Lower Gallery 2s. Second Price 1s.—Upper Gallery 1s. Second Price 6d;
The Doors will be opened at HALF paft FIVE, and the Play begin at HALF paft SIX.
Places for the Boxes to be taken of Mr BRANDON, at the Box-Office, Hart-ftreet, from Ten till Four.
Printed by E. Macleifh, 2, Bow-ftreet, London

On Friday, the Comedy of The POOR GENTLEMAN.
Sir Robert Bramble by Mr. TERRY, Sir Charles Cropland, Mr. FARLEY
Frederick by Mr. VINING,
(From the Theatre Royal, Norwich, being his firft appearance at this Theatre.)
Lieut. Worthington, Mr. BARRYMORE, Ollapod *(with a Song)* Mr FAWCETT,
Corporal Fofs Mr BLANCHARD, Stephen Harrowby Mr EMERY, Humph. Dobbins Mr Simmons
The Hon. Mifs Mac Tab by Mrs. KENNEDY, Emily Worthington, Mrs GIBBS.
After which, *(by particular defire)* the Burlefque Tragick Opera of BOMBASTES FURIOSO.

opportunity presented—Shakespearean tragedies, modern comedies and musical farces.² This evening she has a ticket for *The Clandestine Marriage*, a comedy by the great Shakespearean actor David Garrick and George Colman the elder. *Midas*, by Kane O'Hara, was a burletta or parody of the Italian comic opera and regularly performed as an afterpiece. Both plays dated to the 1760s and were often revived.

One attraction of this latest production was to be Daniel Terry, who had made his Covent Garden debut just a few days earlier and was now stepping into the role of Lord Ogleby in *The Clandestine Marriage*. Terry's name would soon be closely and publicly associated with that of Walter Scott, several of whose novels he adapted or 'Terryfied' for the stage with great success. His forte was said to be comic characters, especially old men. If so, Austen was unimpressed by Terry's interpretation of the elderly Lord Ogleby, writing the next morning to Cassandra: 'Henry thinks he may do; but there was no acting more than moderate.'³ To brother Frank, ten days later, her opinion has hardened into severe general verdict: 'I believe the Theatres are thought at a low ebb at present.'⁴ She was, as her comments on other productions over the years attest, a keen stage critic.

The Clandestine Marriage was a favourite with her, its title possibly dropped into her teenage story 'Love and Freindship',⁵ while elements of the play bear comparison with situations explored in *Mansfield Park*, which she had in draft by September 1813. Despite its condemnation of private theatricals, the novel is everywhere indebted to theatre. Its quiet heroine Fanny Price is both spectator and unwilling centre-stage performer who never does quite play the role expected of her.

To Cassandra next morning she provides more detail: 'We had very good places in the Box next the Stage box—front and 2^d row, the three old ones behind of course … the boxes were fitted up with Crimson velvet.' The Theatre Royal, Covent Garden, was one of two London theatres licensed for spoken dramatic performances during the normal season (the other being Drury Lane); it had been refurbished after a disastrous fire in 1808 burnt it down. The high prices of its renovated private and dress boxes led to riots at the reopening. There was further redecoration in 1813. With a capacity of 3,000, excluding standing room, a grand staircase flanked by porphyry columns and lit by Grecian-style lamps leading to the boxes, and a yellow marble bust of Shakespeare mounted in the anteroom, it was sumptuous.[6] And there we find her on the evening of 15 September with brothers Henry and Edward, seated in the second row of the box next to the stage box, behind her nieces, luxuriating upon rich crimson velvet.

Bound playbill for *The Clandestine Marriage*: John Johnson Collection, Playbills Covent Garden, 1813–1814, Bodleian Libraries, Oxford.

22

Front door, 50 Albemarle Street, London

Did Jane Austen step inside this door? A wall is 'mute' but a door 'speaks', wrote the pioneering sociologist Georg Simmel.[1] Where Chawton Cottage's unoiled hinges spoke with a purposeful creak, alerting the writer to an intrusion on her privacy, No. 50 Albemarle Street boasted the smoothest articulation of any public portal in literary London. When in town, Lord Byron sauntered through it most days. Since the spring of 1814 he had been a near neighbour at the Albany on Piccadilly with an open invitation to the soirées, held from two to five in the afternoon, in John Murray's elegant first-floor drawing rooms.

By 1815 every ambitious author aspired to be on Murray's list. In London in the autumn of that year, Austen wrote to him 'on the subject of the MS of <u>Emma</u> now in your hands'.[2] Negotiations were at a delicate stage. Would she join Byron, Walter Scott, Tom Moore, Robert Southey, the brilliant Germaine de Staël and numerous

social and political luminaries, most long forgotten, in No. 50's drawing rooms? Suggesting that 'A short conversation may perhaps do more than much Writing', Austen invited Murray to call on her at 23 Hans Place, Chelsea, on the far side of Green Park. Did he call? Murray was, by now, rather grand to be treated as a tradesman by a provincial nobody. But did *she* ever call on *him*?

The product of a less censorious age, Austen has come to us, after circumspect family curation, swaddled in Victorian womanly values—modest, retiring, artless in her unforced instinct as a writer. Her brother Henry, as opportunistic as any in Murray's circle, described her in 1833 as shunning all literary gatherings: 'To her truly delicate mind such display would have given pain instead of pleasure.'[3] So, no, perish the thought; she never crossed the famous threshold.

There are, though, other ways to read the evidence. On the spot to see each novel through the press, she combined proofreading with shopping expeditions. On her own account and with niece Fanny, she made repeated visits in late 1815 to Bond Street, already the luxury retail street it is today. Robert Birchall's, for sheet music, at 133 New Bond Street, was five minutes' walk from 50 Albemarle Street. Would not curiosity, if nothing more, take her to the famous door?

Perhaps, after all, she did cross its threshold. The upstairs drawing rooms were not its only accessible spaces. The ground floor of No. 50 was fitted up for business with writing tables and an accounts department. Either here or in domestic quarters above, family members made manuscript copies, including of Byron's *Manfred* in 1817.[4] Among the copyists was Murray's wife, Anne Elliot, daughter of an Edinburgh bookseller. Does the name sound familiar? Austen took it for her most literary heroine in her last completed novel, *Persuasion*, published by Murray in 1818. The compliment gives added force to Austen's Anne's remark, 'Men have had every advantage of us ... the pen has been in their hands' (ch. 23). It raises the hint of a possibility: might Austen have joined an alternative ladies' salon inside No. 50?

Running from fashionable Mayfair into Piccadilly, Albemarle Street was laid out at the end of the seventeenth century as residences. Standing four storeys high, No. 50 was built around 1715. John Murray, a second-generation publisher, set up here in 1812, joining the drift westward from the City, where booksellers had been installed since medieval times. Hatchard's was (and still is) on Piccadilly and Thomas Hookham's famous reading rooms were on Old Bond Street. Murray secured No. 50 with his copyrights of two of the period's runaway successes—Maria Rundell's *Domestic Cookery* (1806) and Scott's verse romance *Marmion* (1808).

23

Emma, the Windsor Castle copy

Jane Austen might well have agreed that if writing is an art, publishing is a business. *Emma*, her fourth and last lifetime publication, appeared in late December 1815, with an 1816 date on the title page. She and her new publisher, John Murray, were eager that the novel should make a splash.

With Lord Byron on his list, Murray was the most sought-after publisher of the age. Coincidentally, Austen learned that another notorious celebrity, the Prince Regent, admired her novels and would be pleased to offer his patronage. This unsought honour brought a visit, on 13 November 1815, to Carlton House, the Regent's London residence, and permission to 'dedicate any future Work to HRH the P.R.'[1]

She allocated twelve presentation copies of *Emma*, with a thirteenth bound at her own expense (at the hefty cost of 24 shillings) in red morocco gilt for her royal dedicatee, joking to Cassandra, on

26 November, that the copies were to be 'dispersed among my near Connections—beginning with the P.R. & ending with Countess Morley'.[2]

From this moment, worlds collided. It is unlikely Austen had changed her opinion of the Regent since 16 February 1813 when she wrote to Martha Lloyd of his very public rupture with his wife, Caroline of Brunswick: 'Poor Woman, I shall support her as long as I can, because she is a Woman, & because I hate her Husband.'[3] There are other no less disturbing collisions: '3 or 4 Families in a Country Village', the neighbourhood of *Emma* and her usual provincial subject matter, sits oddly with an appeal to the louche leader of London and Brighton high society.[4]

Not since the teenage squib 'Jack & Alice', where an ambitious young woman inveigles an elderly duke into marriage and her equally calculating sister aspires 'to the affections of some Prince',[5] had she so assiduously courted the aristocracy. Ungainly Lord Osborne in *The Watsons*, imperious Lady Catherine de Bourgh (daughter of an earl), the Dowager Viscountess, Lady Dalrymple, in *Persuasion*, her 'broad back' her single noteworthy feature (ch. 20)—such figures scarcely inject glamour into Austen's fictional landscape.[6] As for the Regent: he is as unwelcome an intruder into *Emma* as the turkey thief into Mrs Weston's poultry house, the alarming incident on which the novel closes.

It is difficult to avoid the verdict that Austen sacrificed scruples, artistic and political, for commercial advantage. What rescues the situation is humour: the vacuous, repetitive form of the dedication to 'HRH the P.R.' recalling the teenage writer's comic contortions in pursuit of patronage.

Publication imminent, she informed Murray, 11 December: 'The Title page must be, Emma, Dedicated by Permission to H.R.H. The

Prince Regent'. Within hours she received his reply, prompting from her this further note: 'As to my direction about the title-page, it was arising from my ignorance only, and from my having never noticed the proper place for a dedication. I thank you for putting me right.'[7] Why did she, by now an experienced published author, make this mistake?

Emma is her only adult novel to hold a dedication. Dedications lie outside the works they usher in. Nonetheless, they perform a gatekeeping function, influencing how we read what follows. The Regent's patronage, it would seem, transported Austen back to her mock-solemn teenage impersonation of the protocols of the professional writer, among which were hyperbolic dedications. These, too, on occasion, were squashed up against the title.

From Carlton House the Regent's copy found its way to the Royal Library, Windsor Castle. But Austen need not have worried about any taint by association. A catalogue mark confirms the novel was demoted for a period to the servants' hall, while its remarkably clean condition suggests it lay unread above and below stairs.

Did royal patronage help sales? Of the 2,000 copies of *Emma* printed, 539 were remaindered at two shillings each in 1820.[8]

Jane Austen
Sarah Hodges
Pay Mackintosh & Co. or Order
Per Pro. of Heath & Co.
Henry Nancy
R. Mackintosh
Harrison

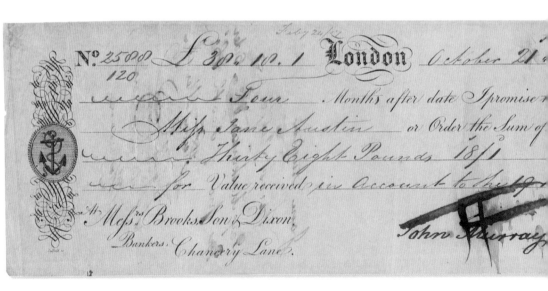

Feby 24 51

N.º 2500   £ 38 . 10 . 1   **London**   October 21

120

Four   Months after date I promise

Miss Jane Austen   or Order the Sum of

Thirty Eight Pounds 18/1

for Value received in Account to the 19

At Mess.rs Brooks, Son & Dixon,

Bankers, Chancery Lane.

John Murray

24

A life in banknotes

Jane Austen and money go together. When, in *Pride and Prejudice*, Jane Bennet asks her sister how long she has loved Mr Darcy, Elizabeth replies: 'I believe I must date it from my first seeing his beautiful grounds at Pemberley' (ch. 59). Readers have tried ever since to explain away that sentence. But the truth is Austen wrote novels that endorse the values of her and our commercial society. She makes acquisitiveness appear principled, by serving up that headiest of romantic cocktails, love and money—the seductive fantasy that we might have it all, mischievously inverted in W.H. Auden's 'the amorous effects of "brass"'.[1]

Her lifetime earnings of around £630 were modest by any contemporary standard; writing never provided her with financial independence.[2] Despite mounting esteem, she earned far less than contemporaries Frances Burney, Maria Edgeworth and Walter Scott, all now by comparison little read. 'The Rich are always respectable', Austen quipped.[3] She, too, has always been respectable, but she would surely have relished the irony that with her face on the Bank of England £10 note, she at last has what she craved: fame *and* money.

So, here are three objects for one, lest we forget what Jane Austen knew: that without money there can be little happiness. The truth is: Jane Austen has always been right on the money.

Henry Austen, Jane's brother, established himself as army agent and banker in London in 1801, forming partnerships there with Henry Maunde and James Tilson, and with satellite country banks, including Gray and Vincent in Alton, Hampshire. There was little regulation of private banks at this time. An unissued note (below) from the Alton Bank names a second Austen investor, Henry's brother Frank. Between 1750 and 1921 local banks issued their own notes, as some Scottish banks still do today.

Long before this, in 1792, the sixteen-year-old Jane dedicated 'Lesley-Castle' to Henry, who added a postscript to her dedication, as follows: 'Messrs Demand & Co— please to pay Jane Austen Spinster the sum of one

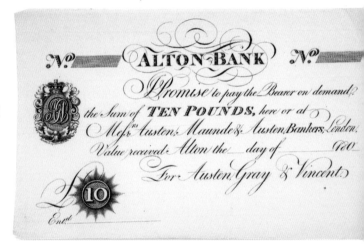

hundred guineas on account of your Humbl. Servant. H.T. Austen. £105:0.0.'[4] Henry's promise of extravagant financial reward taps into a theme running through his sister's teenage writings: virtue is not enough; without money 'a Girl of Genius & Feeling' is at the mercy of every social injustice.[5] Banknotes, often dubiously acquired, are plentiful in these early stories.

Henry opened his bank at 10 High Street, Alton (about 2 miles from Chawton), in 1806. This note can be dated between 1807 and 1815. Always a chancer, Henry was declared bankrupt in March 1816, during the post-war financial slump. The note became worthless and Jane, with other family members, lost her deposits. Bought by Jane Austen's House at auction in February 1989, the note's purchase price was £160.

Pictured at the start of this entry is a cancelled cheque for the sum of £38, 18 shillings and 1 penny made out from John Murray to 'Miss Jane Austin'. Repeating the misspelling, Austen has signed the back 'Jane Austin'. At a time when Walter Scott, the bestselling novelist of the age, was clearing annual profits of £10,000, this modest sum was all she received on sales of *Emma*, her fourth novel, a year after publication.

Though dated October 21st 1816, Murray's cheque was a four-month bill, not cashable until February 1817. Money was tight and, in order to bank it straightaway, Jane Austen had no option but to discount it at a loss, as details on the back show.[6]

On 14 September 2017 the Bank of England issued the first polymer £10 banknote. A stylized Jane Austen's face was chosen to adorn the back. The twelve-sided writing table used at Chawton Cottage also features in the note's design. The year 2017 marked the 200th anniversary of Austen's death. She is only the third female (other than Elizabeth II, who appeared from 1960) to feature on a Bank of England note: Florence Nightingale featured on the £10 note from 1975 to 1992; Elizabeth Fry, the Quaker prison reformer, on the £5 note between 2002 and 2016. The Bank of England polymer £10 could be in your pocket.

25

Jane Austen's pelisse

This silk pelisse can be dated between 1812 and 1814. It is believed to have been worn and owned by Jane Austen. While her wardrobe included more than one pelisse made from wool for ordinary wear, it is likely that she had only one made of silk. This may be the very garment that, on 24 August 1814, she requested her sister Cassandra to send by carrier to her in London: 'Henry ... has once mentioned ... calling on the Birches & the Crutchleys ... I must provide for the possibility, by troubling you to send up my Silk Pelisse.'[1]

Originally a short military cloak, the pelisse was adapted as fashionable women's wear around 1790–1810, when it became a long, fitted coat-dress with set-in sleeves and empire-line waist. Many Regency examples retained traces of their military inspiration, such as frog fastenings and braid trim.

Clothing has a long history of incorporating symbolism.[2] That woven into the fabric of Austen's pelisse—twilled brown English silk sarcenet sprinkled over with a gold falling oak leaf pattern—represents a compliment to the oak ships and stout hearts of Britain's

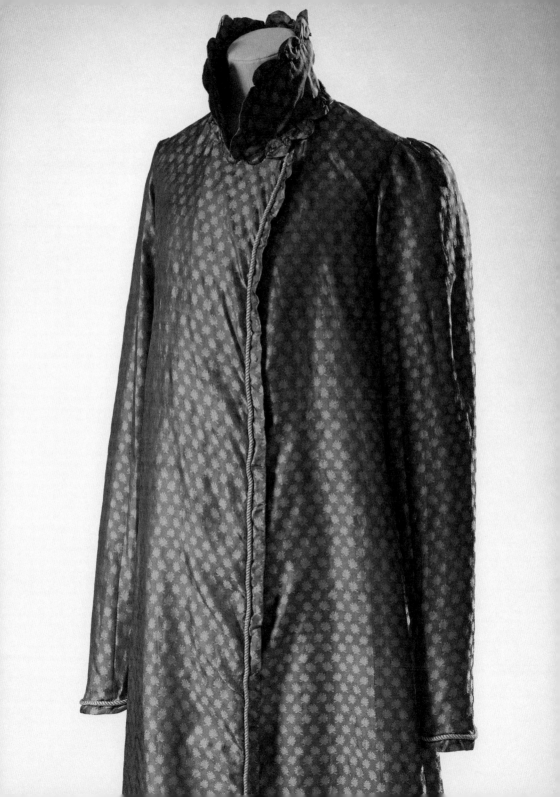

navy. The song 'Heart of Oak', composer William Boyce and lyricist the celebrated actor David Garrick, dates from 1759, a year of great naval victories. War has regularly inspired domestic fashion. With Britain engaged in a prolonged European war, wearing this garment in the 1810s was a patriotic gesture. Naval officers (Austen's brothers Frank and Charles among them) were national heroes and figures of glamour. A hundred years later, early in the First World War, full calf-length skirts dubbed 'war crinoline' were all the rage; so, too, military-style tunic jackets and the trench coat, practical as well as fashionable attire for women and men.

Austen's adult life was lived in the shadow of war. If we have failed to notice how her fiction registers wartime, it is because her perspective is that of the women who wait at home for letters from brothers or husbands campaigning overseas, and who, like her heroine Anne Elliot in *Persuasion*, scour the Navy Lists and newspapers for notice of men killed and officers promoted (ch. 4). Austen can claim to be our first novelist of the home front.

In Austen's day, before off-the-peg mass manufacture, outer garments (as opposed to shirts and underclothes) were bespoke, made to fit the contours of one particular wearer. Though Austen was herself an excellent sewer, the expensive fabric and complex cut of the sleeves declare this pelisse to have been professionally made. With a high value for a wearer of Austen's social rank and modest means, its modern equivalent might be a garment designed by Vivienne Westwood, Chanel or Versace. The pelisse suggests Austen allowed herself a treat around 1813 when profits from her novels permitted some modest financial independence.

If we rarely hear how her characters dress, Austen's personal correspondence is a rich source of information about her shopping habits, her interest in fashion and her thrift as a woman of slender means used to mending and recycling garments.[3] Sad to say, this glamorous pelisse may not have been much worn.

Clothing is a material text to be read and interpreted much like one of Austen's novels. The woman who wore this close-fitting pelisse was slender and, for her time, tall: around 1.70 metres (5 foot 7 inches). The pelisse may have been gifted after Jane's death to her brother Edward's family. His daughter Marianne Knight, she of the satin dancing slippers (see Object 5), gave it around 1875 to a family friend, Miss Eleanor Glubbe, who later returned it to the Austen family. The pelisse was then handed down through the family until 1993, when it was donated to the Hampshire Museums Service (now Hampshire Cultural Trust).

26

The Octagon Room, Bath

All three of Jane Austen's Bath novels appeared posthumously; yet Bath is the beginning, middle and end of her writing career. A version of *Northanger Abbey* was sold from Bath to a London publisher in 1803; the unfinished work *The Watsons* was drafted while she was living in Bath in 1804–5; *Persuasion*, her last completed novel, was published with *Northanger Abbey* at the end of 1817, six months after her death. An aerial view, perhaps from a Montgolfier balloon, would disclose Bath, its streets, its Lower and Upper Assembly Rooms, the Pump Room, its coaching inns and abbey, as one interlocking Austen object: compact enough, despite its rapid eighteenth-century development, to be known from end to end by a keen pedestrian, such as she, undaunted by its hilly aspect. After her father's death in 1805, his copy of *Excursions from Bath* (1801), by the Revd Richard Warner, passed into Jane's collection.[1] Unlike London, the city's Georgian footprint defines it even now. We might still imagine Austen or Anne Elliot walking there.

When the Austens arrived in May 1801 the fashionable spa town was already a little passé, overtaken by seaside resorts with royal patronage, such as Weymouth and Brighton. But for a gentry family with limited means and two ageing unmarried daughters (Jane was twenty-five, Cassandra twenty-eight), Bath, less bound by the strict social divisions operating in London, offered suitable opportunities. The first twenty of *Northanger Abbey*'s thirty-one chapters are set in its streets and public rooms or on walks and in carriage drives around Bath. Later, in *Persuasion*, the city's faded charms make the perfect setting for Anne Elliot, past her first bloom, and for Sir Walter, whose improvidence has wasted his estate. This final novel discloses the town's subtly graduated economics: the best streets to rent houses; the places to be seen and those it is wiser to avoid, like Mrs Smith's lowly lodgings in Westgate Buildings. It's in the upmarket shopping district of Milsom Street (pictured right) that Anne, turning into Molland's confectioner's to avoid the rain, bumps into Captain Wentworth.

The fashionable Upper or New Assembly Rooms, opening in 1771, consisted of a card room, a ball room, a tea room, doing double duty as a concert room, and the Octagon Room, a space for circulating, named for its eight-sided shape. Here, waiting by one of its four marble fireplaces, Anne Elliot meets Captain Wentworth and they have at last what the narrator calls an 'interesting, almost too interesting conversation' (ch. 20). At around 14 metres across (46 feet), the Octagon is the average size of a theatre stage, with a door from the main entrance and another into the concert room, effectively bisecting the space.[2] Their encounter exploits its theatrical potential. Wentworth enters, Anne moves forward and speaks, causing Wentworth to redirect his steps from the straight line between outer and inner doors until they stand together, downstage. After conventional greetings, they become absorbed in conversation, while upstage Sir Walter and Elizabeth, Anne's father and sister, whisper and watch. The intensity is broken by another entrance from outside: that of Lady Dalrymple and her daughter, attended by Mr Elliot and Colonel Wallis. As they step downstage, in their turn, to fawn upon their aristocratic cousins, Sir Walter and Elizabeth divide Anne from Captain Wentworth, bringing her towards his rival Mr Elliot. When Anne turns to rejoin Wentworth he has exited into the concert room. She can only follow.

In a movement suited to Austen's most abstracted heroine, the scene now shifts from the Octagon's social bustle to Anne's 'happiness … from within' as public space yields to intimate space, performance to reflection, and the conclusion that 'He must love her.' The episode is a powerful demonstration of Austen's superb stagecraft.

27

The donkey carriage

'He suggested that an excursion to Mars in his private rocket
might prove agreeable.'

Stella Gibbons, 'Jane in Space', *Punch*, 1960

Long before *Pride and Prejudice and Zombies* (2009), 'Jane in Space'
recodes the Austen village as a mixed-species community of
humans, Venusians and Martians living close by a rocket station.
With the joyously parodic *Cold Comfort Farm* (1933) behind her,
Gibbons riffs stylishly on the ingredients of the classic Austen
novel—small-town social rituals, marriageable heroine, the eligible
stranger who rents a nearby estate setting local hearts a-flutter:
Rocket-Commander Smasher, 'a monster—of debauchery'.

Though she drew the line at space rockets, the teenage Austen
enumerated several improbable means of transport enjoyed by
Mr Clifford of Bath in the comic story she dedicated to her nine-
year-old brother Charles. 'He had a Coach, a Chariot, a Chaise,
a Landeau, a Landeaulet, a Phaeton, a Gig, a Whisky, an italian

Chair, a Buggy, a Curricle & a wheel barrow.'[1] Overlook the absurd-
ity of scale, and here are some of the ingredients that make up
the immersive pleasure of Austen's adult novels. Like card games
and dance steps, the fine differences between a landeaulet and a
phaeton expand her novels' affective reach, contributing to their
illusion of authenticity for her enraptured readers.

As for Austen herself, in 1891 the pioneer American biographer
Oscar Fay Adams speculated on her visit by stagecoach to Scotland.
He found evidence in a letter of 23 August 1814 describing her
journey to London in an overcrowded vehicle: 'it put me in mind',
she wrote there, 'of my own Coach between Edinburgh & Sterling'.[2]
Not until 1922 and the first appearance in print of the teenage
road-trip story 'Love and Freindship' was this unlikely detail transposed from biography into art.

So, no trips by coach to Edinburgh or by rocket into space, but
how far might she have travelled in this wooden donkey carriage?
The simplest and cheapest form of transport, it was probably made
locally soon after the Austen women settled at Chawton in 1809. It
required no stabling and avoided vehicle tax.[3] The donkey could
graze in the orchard field that in those days lay beyond the garden.
Her niece Caroline remembered that her grandmother 'seldom
used it', but 'Aunt Jane found it a help to herself in getting to
Alton.'[4] A donkey's walking pace, at 4 miles per hour, is little more
than that of an energetic walker; the short journey to Alton for
shopping would take around thirty minutes by donkey.

A boxed bench seat provides just enough room for two people
with a space beneath for parcels. Hooks on the shafts serve to
couple the harness. When in harness, the seat is centred exactly
above the axle, minimizing the weight the donkey has to pull. With
no brakes, the carriage only stops when the donkey stops. Nothing

romantic or pastoral about it: we can be sure that this unsprung cart was extremely uncomfortable, especially during Austen's final illness, on the rutted lanes around Chawton.

She described using it in July 1816, but harsh weather prevented even local trips the following December, when 'the walk is beyond my strength'.[5] By March 1817 she planned to ride the donkey rather than harness the carriage.[6] As for the donkeys: 'our Donkeys are necessarily having so long a run of luxurious idleness that I suppose we shall find that they have forgotten much of their Education when we use them again.'[7]

A gift to Jane Austen's House in May 1950 from Alison, Lady Bradford, a Knight family relation, the cart was given to her by Montagu Knight (see Object 19). The carriage was restored in 1998, after inspection by the Head Carriage Restorer to Queen Elizabeth II.

28

A lock of hair

Death came at half past four on the morning of 18 July 1817.
Soon afterwards, Cassandra Austen cut several locks of Jane's
hair for family and friends. On 28 July she sent hair to Anne
Sharp, former governess to Edward Knight's children; niece
Fanny Knight chose an oval brooch to hold her lock; Cassandra
had another made into a ring for herself; a lock was later given to
Harriet Palmer, sister-in-law and in 1820 second wife to widowed
Charles Austen; others, too, now untraced, were distributed. In
the testamentary letter disposing of her possessions after death,
Cassandra bequeathed to Charles's daughter Cassandra: 'Two
rings which I always wear, one her Aunt Jane's hair set in Pearls,
the other her own Mother's hair & her first Aunt Franks in
gold.' There was hair of the living, too, to be given to Charles's
daughter Harriet Jane: 'a square gold broche, without any
inscription, containing Hair,—your own & Franks.'[1]

The lock of hair is an intimate token—John Donne's 'bracelet
of bright hair about the bone'.[2] Worn on the body as brooch or

ring, it binds the dead to the living in sacred association. Set inside Edward Ferrars' ring in *Sense and Sensibility* (chs 18 and 22), the lock provides a little plot subterfuge. Hair is a real attribute of someone once here, whom we wish to hold close, but now gone and over time increasingly distant, despite its too tangible presence. What about when the personal link is broken, when Cassandra, her brothers, their wives and her nieces are all gone, when personal history gives way to cultural memory? These are questions I believe we should ask when a token such as this is fated to become museum exhibit. They are also appropriate to the times in which Austen lived: the Romantics were a hair-obsessed lot.

Several hair 'libraries' date from the period. Leigh Hunt, poet friend of Keats and Shelley, built a collection (now at the Harry Ransom Center, Austin, Texas) whose star item is a lock from John Milton's head. The collection at Harvard's Houghton Library includes samples from John Keats, Fanny Brawne, Lady Emma Hamilton, Emily Dickinson, and a lock of Shakespeare's, 'authenticated' by the Romantic forger William Henry Ireland. Mary Shelley kept locks from the living and as mementos of the dead (her mother Mary Wollstonecraft, her poet husband), much of it now in the Bodleian Library, Oxford. Lord Byron, great hair trickster, foisted onto importunate lovers others' hair as his own and stole, from the Bibliotheca Ambrosiana, Milan, a single golden strand from the head of Lucretia Borgia.[3] Sotheby's occasionally auctions celebrity hair, a lock of Beethoven's selling for £35,000 on 11 June 2019.

This lock, that given by Cassandra to Harriet Palmer, now faded from the 'darkish brown' her niece remembered, is in the Jane Austen's House collection.[4] Sold in the 1920s by Charles's granddaughters, it was bought at Sotheby's in 1948 by American enthusiast Alberta H. Burke. At the Jane Austen Society meeting on 23 July 1949 T. Edward Carpenter, founder of the newly opened Jane Austen's House, lamented the loss of so many relics to America. Burke, who was present and outraged by the implications of his remark, leaped to her feet to say she had purchased the hair and would donate it to the Society.[5] In 1950 it was encased in this reeded circular brass frame with a ribbon bow crest by London jeweller Hancock's of Vigo Street.

What does the lock signify now? Burke built her collection of Austen holograph letters, first editions and scrapbooks of ephemera (since divided between the Morgan Library, New York, and Goucher College, Baltimore, Maryland) from a desire to feel close to her favourite author. The hair is emblematic of Austen's intimately entwined Anglo-American commemoration.

29
Dining-room grate

Following the death of Jane's sister Cassandra in 1845, the house in which the Austen women had lived was divided into three tenements for Chawton estate workers. By the 1920s it was in need of modernization. Miss Dorothy Darnell, local resident and lifelong Austen enthusiast, described how walking by the house one day she came across 'the cast-iron grate from the Austens' dining parlour lying on the scrap-heap by the local forge. It had been wrenched out to make way for a gas fire, and its future was uncertain.'¹ The sight led in May 1940 to the formation of the Jane Austen Society and in 1946 an appeal in *The Times* to save the house for the nation. In the meantime, Miss Darnell contacted the Curtis Museum in nearby Alton, which took the grate into safekeeping.

In a letter of June 1948 Elizabeth Jenkins, novelist, Austen biographer and a founder member of the Society, worked up the story of the discarded grate with high-minded disdain for the vulgar comforts of the living. She wrote to congratulate

Mr T. Edward Carpenter, a London lawyer, who had bought the house for £3,000 in response to the Society's appeal:

> I have been thinking so much in the last two or three days of the first time I saw the house—in 1938, long before I had met the Darnells. It was a frosty January day and I walked out from Alton, full of such excitement. A good deal of this was dashed by the conditions I saw. A ruin, full of bats and cobwebs, would have been perfectly acceptable: what was so dreadful was the new gas fire glittering like a set of fake teeth of the worst kind, the larger-than-life size photographs, bull dogs in sailor hats, bamboo tables, pampas grass and loud incessant wireless. As I had just seen Haworth, the contrast was heart breaking. Then, there seemed [no] prospect of anything being done! This is very pleasant to look back on now![2]

In *Orlando* (1928), her fantasy biography, Virginia Woolf pinpointed the moment when a house, adapted over generations to its owners' changing tastes, becomes a house museum:

> everywhere were little lavender bags to keep the moth out and printed notices, 'Please do not touch', which, though she had put them there herself, seemed to rebuke her. The house was no longer hers entirely, she sighed. It belonged to time now; to history; was past the touch and control of the living.[3]

There is a view that 'tourists travel to actual destinations to experience virtual places'.[4] House museums are biographies in brick and stone where all kinds of mundane material things perform spiritual duties. Formally opened to the public on 23 July 1949, the museum, administered by the Jane Austen Memorial Trust, was at first confined to what had been the Austens' drawing room. Other rooms, including that considered by tradition as Jane and Cassandra's bedroom, could be visited by permission of the tenants. Quickly, the careful reconstruction of Jane Austen's House around the restored eighteenth-century dining-room grate fitted the image of a novelist of home and hearth, urgently relevant to Britain's recovery in the late 1940s. Not only was this the very grate where Jane had made the family breakfast of tea and toast—hadn't she also kept our home fires burning through two world wars?

For Carpenter the house was a double memorial: to the novelist who once lived there and to his son, Lieutenant John Philip Carpenter, killed in action on 30 June 1944. By 1953 the tenants had been rehoused; we don't know what became of the modern gas fire.

30

A sermon scrap

In just twenty-eight words, this scrap tells us how marketable
relics of Jane Austen had become by 1870, partly thanks to
the phenomenal success of her nephew James Edward Austen-
Leigh's *A Memoir of Jane Austen*, the first major biography. The
available spoils were so scarce, Austen-
Leigh was soon obliging autograph
hunters with portions of one of his
father's sermons, affixing to each the
information: 'This is the hand writing,
not the composition, of my Aunt,
Jane Austen, Authoress of Pride &
Prejudice.'

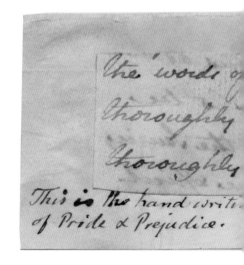

He sent one, by request, to the
Guernsey Mechanics Institute. To his
daughter he confided that 'Mamma'
had found the sermon and that he
was 'able to break it up into about

a manuscript Sermon, of which
She had written out a great deal
for my father in 1814. I inclose
a Specimen. with an attestation
of its genuineness

I am
Yours faithfully
Rev.ᵈ Austen Leigh

em may get into a habit of repeating
e Prayers by rote, perhaps without
rdeastanding — certainly without
ling their full force & meaning.

not the composition. of my Aunt, Jane Austen, Author of
Jᵒ Edwᵈ Austen Leigh

twenty sentences', pasting 'each on a large strip of paper' and adding 'a certificate' to authenticate the hand.[1]

The sermon can be dated to 1814. This scrap reads: 'Men may get into a habit of repeating the words of our Prayers by rote, perhaps without thoroughly understanding—certainly without thoroughly feeling their full force & meaning.' It reminds us of Jane Austen's religious convictions: she was an Anglican, the daughter, sister and aunt of Anglican clergymen. The scrap echoes a discussion in *Mansfield Park* (ch. 34) on the 'art of reading' and its importance to the modern clergyman. *Mansfield Park*, an intensely serious novel in which religion serves a public/political interest, was published in May 1814. Perhaps the scrap demonstrates the cross-fertilization between Austen's creative writing and the wider life of her family, raising the possibility that, if she copied out James's sermon, her novel inspired his themes.

From a correspondence of possibly thousands, only 161 of Austen's letters have made it into print, and the originals of several of these are missing. Quickly, her autograph became valuable by its rarity: 'I have hardly ever seen a collection in which Byron is not represented or one in which Jane Austen is', Lady Charnwood, a major twentieth-century collector, noted in 1930.[2]

Some letters were, like those of the contemporary poet John Keats, submitted to the scissors. Her niece Anna Lefroy divided one, dated 29 November 1814, into five (possibly more) portions, at least one of which has not so far resurfaced, while two others—one no more than a date, the other its closing salutation—were bagged by Lady Charnwood and are now in the British Library's Charnwood Collection.[3] In 1841 Catherine

Hutton of Birmingham, an avid amateur collector, who according to her own estimate possessed 'upward of 2000' autographs, expressed herself content with a signature—'Yours very affect:^{ly} / J. Austen / Chawton Wednesday / Feb. 17'—obtained circuitously from Jane's brother Frank. One hundred years later when Hutton's album was broken up, the signature was bought for $25 by William Clay of Rochester, New York State. It is all that appears to have survived of a letter possibly further divided, like so many others, to appease the autograph trade.[4]

Scraps in Austen's hand on occasion turn up making headline news, like the final six lines (no signature) of a letter written 15–16 September 1813, discovered in an autograph album auctioned in September 2017, their text unrecorded in any print edition. What do they contain?—a reference to the inventory Jane has made of brother Henry's linen store.[5] To the collector, the scriptural gesture alone appears sufficient, regardless of what is written. It is enough to possess the loved hand's trace upon paper.

This sermon scrap, affixed to its certificate of authentication, was purchased for £11,000 by Jane Austen's House in 2013. It was pasted into a first-edition copy of Austen-Leigh's *Memoir* with his accompanying letter to the Revd G. Berkeley. Other scraps from the sermon occasionally come onto the market.[6]

Her charm to children was great sweetness of
manner. She seemed to love you, & you loved
her naturally in return — This as well as I can
now recollect & analyse, was what I felt in my
earliest days, before I was old enough to understand
her cleverness. But soon came the delight
of her playful talk — Everything she could make
amusing to a child — Then, as I got older, &
when cousins came to share the entertainment,
she would tell us the most delightful stories
chiefly of invention, & her fairies had all characters
of their own — The tale was invented, I am sure of
the moment, & has sometimes continued for 2 or 3
days. I occasion served —

As to my Aunt's personal appearance hers has
the first face that I can remember thinking pretty
not that I used that word to myself, but I
know I looked at her with admiration —
Her face was rather round than long — She had
bright, but not a pink colour — a clear brown
complexion

31

Caroline Austen, 'My Aunt Jane Austen', 1867

There are the male biographers: brother Henry, nephew James Edward Austen-Leigh and, in the twentieth century, William and Richard Arthur Austen-Leigh, son and grandson of James Edward. Their accounts have assumed the status of sourcebooks for the fervid Austen biography industry. But their authority is traceable to hidden histories supplied by the women's communities within which Austen lived day by day. Hidden, because the diverse perspectives of nieces Anna Lefroy, Fanny Knight and Caroline Austen long remained unpublished, homogenized within the official narrative.

Anna Austen (later Lefroy) was sent to Steventon aged two to live with her teenage aunts. Caroline Austen, twelve years younger than half-sister Anna, was only four when, in 1809, her aunts moved into Chawton Cottage. Anna and Caroline each wrote their lively, quirky memories, subsequently damped down inside brother James Edward's clerical prose.

To Caroline we owe the description of Austen's personal appearance in her thirties and her daily routine at Chawton: her early morning piano practice; her superintendence of the household stores of tea, sugar and wine. More surprisingly, we learn of her affinity with children and the stories she invented for them about fairyland ('& her Fairies had all characters of their own').[1] Caroline's is a narrative of inconsequential observation: Aunt Jane playing with cup and ball, her neat satin stitch when sewing, and the makeshift sofa—three chairs arranged together—on which she stoically rested during her final illness. Caroline reported details of the final illness as recorded in the notebooks left by her mother Mary Lloyd Austen, who nursed her sister-in-law in Winchester in the last days. From her mother, too, she passed on emotional colour: Austen's distress at leaving Steventon; her frustrated love affairs. As an unmarried adult, Caroline was Aunt Cassandra's regular companion, receiving more confidences in later years.

Jane Austen is resolved or concentrated in Caroline's reminiscences into the biographemes that most nearly encapsulate the kaleidoscopic fragments that make up any and every life.[2] 'The main of life', wrote Austen's beloved Samuel Johnson, 'is … composed of small incidents.'[3] Caroline's is a discontinuous narrative, a child's point of view retrieved, falteringly, in later life: 'I knew her', she wrote, 'only with a child's knowledge.' In the absence of personal testimony from confessional letters and diaries (though those too will always be subject to fictionalization), the image we have of Jane Austen depends upon others' late reconstruction, the changing viewpoints of invested family members. For a period, from the mid-nineteenth century to the early twentieth, these memories were still in flux, Austenian lore rewritten up to and beyond the verges of romance by female memorialists, several of whom in each generation were also fiction writers, like Anna Lefroy and her daughter Fanny Caroline.

Austen, too, hid trace female biographies deep inside her novels: that of Jane Fairfax the war orphan in *Emma*; the seduced and abandoned Elizas, mother and daughter, in *Sense and Sensibility*; Maria Bertram, the sacrificial offering to her father's ambition in *Mansfield Park*. These women do not tell their own stories. In the interests of composed narrative, official biography can flatten disparate perspectives, voices and kinds of information into a single register, shorn of evidentiary biases and gaps. But evidence operates in two directions: it is only ever meaningful if reattached to the person witnessing as well as she who is witnessed. Jane Austen herself can only ever be a novelistic construct.

Caroline Austen collected her memories of Aunt Jane for family consumption, 'that *she* should not be forgotten by her nearest descendants', writing them out in March 1867, aged sixty-one, fifty years after her aunt's death. Her memoir was not published independently until 1952, after R.A. Austen-Leigh presented the manuscript in 1949 to the Jane Austen Society.[4]

32

The Cobb, Lyme Regis, Dorset

Hallam Tennyson's *Memoir* of his father Alfred, Lord Tennyson records how in the summer of 1867 the poet travelled to Lyme Regis, 'led on ... by the description of the place in Miss Austen's *Persuasion*'. Walking the 9 miles from nearby Bridport, he called on fellow poet Francis Palgrave (he of *The Golden Treasury*) and, 'refusing all refreshment, he said at once: "Now take me to the Cobb, and show me the steps from which Louisa Musgrove fell."'[1] Louisa's fall marks the dramatic mid-point of *Persuasion*, Austen's last completed novel.

A raised stone breakwater, built to protect shipping and the town, the Cobb at Lyme was a visitor attraction long before Louisa Musgrove's incautious leap. Celia Fiennes, late-seventeenth-century traveller, described it as 'like a halfe moon ... raised with a high wall and this runns into the sea a good compass, that the Shipps rides safely within it'.[2] Tennyson's response makes clear that the

Cobb already filled a place in his imagination before he found it on the map, the events of Austen's novel preparing the emotional ground for a real location. 'Led on', he is a secular pilgrim pursuing traces of the beloved author.

He is also a tourist gripped by the intensified engagement that generally marks tourist activities. Jane Austen's lifetime coincided with the rise of middle-class tourism (the word 'tourist' was a recent coinage) and the leisurely enjoyment of beautiful scenery that from the late eighteenth century defined our modern notion of travel for sightseeing. Her very description of the Cobb in *Persuasion* frames it in the jargon of guidebook and holiday brochure: 'the Cobb itself, its old wonders and new improvements, with the very beautiful line of cliffs stretching out to the east of the town, are what the stranger's eye will seek' (ch. 11). One of the characteristics of this way of writing is that it anticipates what is seen, enlisting the senses through reading. To be a tourist is to be a reader. Tennyson arrives at the Cobb with a heart already full of the place he has yet to see.

Emotional anticipation is an article of tourism's compact with the older way of pilgrimage. We find it in Austen's best-loved novel, *Pride and Prejudice*, where it informs Elizabeth Bennet's 'Northern tour', as her quickened response to Pemberley House and its contents shows; and supremely so in the moment when Mr Darcy himself appears before her, a revenant almost, conjured into life through the power of place on Elizabeth's imagination.

Every Austen lover is an Elizabeth Bennet or a Tennyson. In the closing months of the nineteenth century, sisters Constance and Ellen Hill set off through the byways of Hampshire in search of a place they called 'Austen-land', an imagined topography overlaying real ground. They planned a biography: Constance, preparing the text, interviewed the surviving few who had known Jane—among

them the grandson of Jane's hairdresser—while her sister Ellen made sketches (including of the Cobb steps). In pursuit of anecdotes and relics, they described themselves, Tennyson-wise, as invited onwards by 'a sudden ray of light and leading'.[3] Their book has lasting value as a record of scenes and people about to fade from living memory.

Modern guidebooks track Austen across the map—Anne-Marie Edwards's *In the Steps of Jane Austen* and Louise Allen's *Walking Jane Austen's London*. Tour operators offer trips to 'real' Austen locations. Advice manuals propose solutions to life's problems inside a virtual Austen-land: *Jane Austen's Guide to Romance: The Regency Rules*; *Miss Jane Austen's Guide to Modern Life's Dilemmas*. All set the reader in dialogue with the beloved author and in the place where she once stood. Whose ground is more solid? Jane Austen is now just part of the landscape. The descriptor 'Austenland' resurfaced in a film of 2013.

33

Chris Hammond, illustration for *Sense and Sensibility*, 1899

One from a collection illustrating scenes from Austen's first published novel *Sense and Sensibility*, this pen and ink drawing was commissioned by publishers George Allen in 1899 from Chris (Christiana) Hammond (1860–1900). The first English illustrated editions of Austen's novels had appeared in 1833 in Bentley's Standard Novels series. At this stage, images were confined to a modest steel-engraved frontispiece and a second title page with engraved vignette. From 1849 Routledge's Railway Library packaged Austen cheaply to entertain passengers journeying on the relatively new steam trains. They slapped the novels inside covers emblazoned with lurid woodcut illustrations, appealing to the very tastes for mystery and wild romance that she had so thoroughly mocked. By the 1890s there was a booming market in lavishly

"Oh, Elinor! she cried, I have such a
secret to tell you about Marianne"

illustrated editions that, using advances in print technology, placed line drawings within the text, binding illustration more closely to the reading experience.

Chris Hammond was among the most productive working in this intimate new style, illustrating reissues of classic nineteenth-century novels by Maria Edgeworth, William Thackeray and Elizabeth Gaskell as well as Austen's *Emma* (1898) and *Pride and Prejudice* (1899). The style was dubbed the Cranford school, after Hugh Thomson's 1891 illustrated edition of Gaskell's *Cranford*. Thomson had moved on to Austen in 1894. But where Thomson invested Regency-period detail with whimsical nostalgia for a lost pre-industrial society, Hammond injected something bolder, freer and less sentimental. Though still catering to a lucrative conservative taste, her illustrations are less stagey; her figures suggest movement and personality. She nudges a static decorative art towards something more interpretative and psychologically convincing. In conversation, Hammond described how she worked: 'When I am illustrating a story, I read the tale first, and as I read, I see the people all before me, and then I draw them to illustrate the moments of the story that I think most effective. But I cannot be sure that I see the author's creations aright.'[1]

In this scene from chapter 12, Margaret Dashwood informs her eldest sister Elinor of her suspicion that Marianne will soon marry Willoughby. Hammond imbues the small detail with supplementary drama that invites the reader's emotional engagement: Margaret bursts in through the door to find Elinor (Hammond-like?) seated at the table, sketch pad and pencil in hand. Facial expressions appear fleeting while the oblique planes and hatching of the design create an illusion of three-dimensional space. Hammond decided for herself which scenes to illustrate; her sixty-four sketches for *Sense and Sensibility* form a dynamic commentary upon the narrative, subjective and impressionistic in style, and all the more powerful for that.

Active as illustrator in the same years as Kate Greenaway and Beatrix Potter, Hammond's professional skill has gained less recognition. But she worked in interesting company: her Edgeworth illustrations accompanied editions with introductions written by Anne Thackeray Ritchie, Thackeray's daughter and step-aunt to Virginia Woolf. Thackeray Ritchie's essays on Edgeworth and Austen were collected in *A Book of Sybils* (1883), where she described Austen's life as being 'as much made up of minutes as of years'—an allusion not just to its brevity but to the compact nature of her art.[2]

Hammond, who also died young, worked to similar compact scale, capturing Austen's novels, as she said herself, moment by moment. Her original drawings were dispersed and sold before the 1940s. In 2017 twelve were discovered in an attic in New Zealand, part of a family archive belonging to the late Revd Arthur Stanley Moffatt. They were purchased from the family by Jane Austen's House in 2018 with the assistance of the Jane Austen Society.

34

Memorial window, Winchester Cathedral

Hard on her death was born her legend. If much about Jane Austen eludes us, the absence of a definitive face and a documented life has worked to her advantage, easing her passage to posterity and perfection. She was buried on 24 July 1817 in Winchester Cathedral, a site eulogized only five months later by her newly ordained brother, the Revd Henry Austen, as 'in the whole catalogue of its mighty dead' not holding 'the ashes of a brighter genius or a sincerer Christian'.[1] High claim indeed for the church that contains the remains of the ancient Saxon and Norman kings of Wessex and England, Egbert, Canute, his wife Queen Emma, William Rufus, and at one time Alfred the Great, not to mention the shrine of Winchester's early bishop and patron Saint Swithun.

In 1866 an article in *The Englishwoman's Domestic Magazine* expressed frustration with a writer whose image was already so carefully manufactured, so obsessively partial (in both senses) that

'we can think of her as nothing less than an angel writing novels with a quill plucked from one of her own wings, and unfortunately there is no known likeness of her to dissipate the idea.'[2] The ground was prepared for 'St Aunt Jane of Steventon-cum-Chawton Canonicorum', that sacred composite emerging from family-authorized hagiography.

Winchester Cathedral and Austen's Christian deathbed frame her clergyman nephew's *Memoir of Jane Austen* (1870), which opens with a distant memory of himself a young man among the mourners gathered round her grave and closes with her burial beneath a black marble slab 'almost opposite to the beautiful chantry tomb of William of Wykeham', the fourteenth-century Bishop of Winchester and Chancellor of England.[3] By 1870 'England's Jane', as Rudyard Kipling would later name her, had her cult as vigorous as that of any medieval saint. Kipling added the poem to his extraordinary story 'The Janeites' (1924) about Austen worship in the trenches of the Great War:

> Jane lies in Winchester, blessed be her shade!
> Praise the Lord for making her, and her for all she made.
> And, while the stones of Winchester—or Milsom Street—remain,
> Glory, Love, and Honour unto England's Jane![4]

With proceeds from the *Memoir* a brass plaque was mounted in 1872 on the wall above her burial place in the cathedral's north aisle, and in 1900 a public subscription paid for this memorial window dedicated to Jane Austen. The work of the distinguished stained-glass designer and pupil of William Morris, Charles Eamer Kempe, its top panel features St Augustine of Canterbury, patron saint of England, also known as Austin, and on either side are set the coat of arms of the Austen family. Below and centred, King

David plays his harp, and below him a Latin inscription reads 'Remember in the Lord Jane Austen, who died July 18th, A.D. 1817.' Below that Saint John holds a book opened at his Gospel's first phrase, 'In the beginning was the Word.' On the outer panels the sons of Korah hold scrolls of psalm texts. Masculine and religious iconography aplenty, but Jane Austen herself is undepicted, just as her writing life is unrecorded on the marble slab that covers her and proclaims her virtues: 'The benevolence of her heart, the sweetness of her temper, and the extraordinary endowments of her mind.' The plaque makes some small amends, but gives only modest place to 'her writings' as against 'Christian Faith and Piety'.[5]

When central heating was installed in the cathedral in the 1930s her coffin was moved a metre or so to allow for the pipes. We can imagine her now looking askance at the plaque and the window with their glaring omissions.

35

Danish translation of *Pride and Prejudice*, 1904

'Both our Aunts read French easily ... both had some knowledge of Italian', wrote Anna Lefroy.[1] Into how many languages have Jane Austen's novels been translated?[2] Estimates vary from thirty-five to over forty. For some, her quintessential 'Englishness', like her provincialism, proved a barrier only lifted in the twentieth century. There were French translations in her lifetime, including serialized extracts of *Pride and Prejudice* within months of its English publication in 1813. German translations began in 1822, Swedish in 1836, Norwegian in 1871, but Spanish only in 1919 and Italian as late as 1932, after Japanese (1926) and Serbo-Croat (1929). An early dramatization of *Pride and Prejudice*, published in Bombay

...or, at vi nok kommer til at træffe ham paa Soiréerne og

...orestille os for ham" sagde Elizabeth.

Long vil gjøre det, hun har selv to Niecer. Hun er en egen-

...jeg kan ikke fordrage hende."

...Bennet, og jeg er glad over at Du ikke er afhængig af

...g eller ej."

...ham intet Svar, men, ude af Stand til at beherske sig gav

...saa en af sine Døttre.

...blir dog ikke ved med at hoste saadan. — Tag dog en Smule.

...Du sønderriver dem jo!"

...med sine Hosteanfald" sagde hendes Fader. "hun anbringer

...g Tider."

...øjeblic at jeg hoster" sagde Kitty gnavent, naar skal Du igjen

...æs Moder, og da Mrs. Long først kommer hjem Dagen før,

...rende at forestille ham for os, da hun jo ikke kjender ham."

...adelen paa Din Side, idet Du jo saa vil være i Stand til at

...uligt, hvor kan jeg det — jeg kjender ham jo ikke, hvor kan

...?"

..., et fjortendages Bekjendtskab er kun kort, og man ved jo

... Stand virkelig er. Men hvis vi ikke vover det, er der nok

...Alt kommer til Alt vil Mrs. Long og hendes Niecer

...for, da hun vil betragte det som en venlig Handling af Dig naar

...vil jeg tage det paa mig."

...deres Fader. Mrs. Bennet sagde blot:

...nak."

...gen med dette energiske Udraab, spurgte han, behager

... og den Vægt der lægges herpaa som "Snak". Deri er jeg

...ig. Hvad siger Du til det, Mary? Jeg ved Du er en ung

"Jeg haaber Mr. Bingley vil synes om den Lizzy."

(Mumbai) in 1912 was in Marathi. The first Russian translation (*Pride and Prejudice*) was as late as 1967. One of the earliest gifts to Jane Austen's House was a copy of *Persuasion* in Finnish. In the later twentieth century, translations appeared in minority languages: Catalan, Icelandic, Latvian, Estonian, Galician and Basque. Many are of single novels rather than collected editions. Some, especially early on, were appropriated to the expectations of their adopted translator, language and culture.

The only nineteenth-century Danish translation was of *Sense and Sensibility* (*Forstand og Hjerte*, 'Mind and Heart') in 1855–6. A preference for tales of sentiment and historical romances (the novels of Walter Scott and Fenimore Cooper) and some lingering post-Napoleonic antipathy towards Britain may explain why no other Austen novel was published in Danish until *Pride and Prejudice* (*Stolthed og Fordom*) appeared as volume 24 in the 52-volume Gyldendal Bibliotek (1928–30).[3] This handwritten translation of *Pride and Prejudice* is therefore a glorious exception. According to family tradition, it was lovingly prepared in 1904 by two Danish sisters, Dorothea (Bébé) (1866–1946) and Margrethe Fredstrup (1873–1957), as a gift to their mother, who did not speak English.[4]

Distressed gentlewomen of a kind familiar from Austen's life and fiction, the sisters crafted their book while teaching French and needlework at a private girls' school in Nyborg on the Danish island of Funen. Margrethe, a skilled binder, bound its seventeen paper gatherings with cotton thread and satin ribbon ties, encasing them in boards covered in linen, embroidered front and back with vines and flowers. The sisters adorned their translation with meticulous watercolour copies of Charles Edmund Brock's glossy six-colour lithographic plates for *Pride and Prejudice* (Macmillan & Co., 1895)—forty in all. How long must it have taken to execute?

The lost manuscript of *Pride and Prejudice* perhaps wrapped cheese or fish and fed the fire. No manuscripts have survived for the famous six novels, apart from two discarded chapters of *Persuasion*, now in the British Library, London. From this frail survivor and the extant manuscripts of her unfinished writings (*The Watsons* and *Sanditon*), we know that Austen, too, preferred as writing supports homemade booklets that simulated print gatherings.[5]

The Fredstrup sisters' manuscript is a scribal copy of a published work: print retrofitted to writing. As such, it is an embodied memory of a relationship to a loved book and author, an attentive translation in words, images and material structure of a known printed copy. It is both allusive and ultimately elusive: meaningful in the labour that patiently conjured it into existence, yet lacking in significance as manuscript. A piece of fan art, it is a substitute – not a point of origin. Yet the sisters' artisanal skills move Austen's novel from the public back into the private realm. Reinscription and illustration endow their manuscript with surplus pleasure that speaks to and validates their taste and experience. In this sense, like an Austen manuscript, their book has unique specificity. Aase Barner Fredstrup, Bébé and Margrethe's great-niece, donated it to Jane Austen's House in 2015.

36

Jane Austen plate, Charleston, 1932–34

This is one from a collection of fifty hand-decorated plates, an open-ended commission from the art historian Kenneth Clark and his wife Jane. Together they make up the *Famous Women Dinner Service,* completed by Vanessa Bell and Duncan Grant between 1932 and 1934 at Charleston, their Sussex home. Anticipating a high-end service, with tureens, mustard pots and sauce boats, the Clarks in fact received these portrait dinner plates. Plain, white, functional Wedgwood plates (25.5 cm or 10 inches in diameter), they depict twelve writers, twelve dancers and actors, twelve queens and twelve beauties, the final two plates showing Bell and Grant, the only man in the series. A female history is laid out upon everyday domestic objects that also capture the Bloomsbury ethos: challenging divisions between the high and decorative arts and questioning social and sexual arrangements.

Jane Austen

In the unconventional households of Bloomsbury and Charleston, debates around the dinner table on art, literature, politics and economics combined with hospitality and food, fostering links between intellectual freedoms and material things. The plates have been described as seminal in feminist art history.[1] In retrospect, they contest in advance the influential portrait that Kenneth Clark would bring to television screens in 1969—*Civilisation: A Personal View*—an elitist perspective, populated exclusively by white Western males.

Many of the women depicted challenge definitions of history itself. Among the queens, Cleopatra and Jezebel are ranged with British Queen Mary (1867–1953) and a dark-skinned, warrior-like Queen of Sheba. Among the beauties, Helen of Troy shares space with Pocahontas and Miss America 1933 (Marian Bergeron, aged fifteen). Among the writers, George Eliot, the Ancient Greek poet Sapho (*sic*) and the eleventh-century Japanese novelist Murasaki keep company with Jane Austen and Bell's sister Virginia Woolf, whose study of women lost to history, *A Room of One's Own*, had appeared in 1929.[2]

From inside her own irregular Chawton household, Austen may well have found such odd-assorted female company congenial. A late allusion in a letter of 22 May 1817 to her resilient friend Anne Sharp makes clear how she valued 'the power that strong (female) souls must have over weak minds'.[3] Her contemporary Mary Hays, a feminist moving in radical circles, produced a six-volume *Female Biography; or, Memoirs of Illustrious and Celebrated Women, of all ages and countries* (1803). Its 300 entries embrace the ancient (Cynisca, fifth-century CE Spartan princess, first woman to win at the Olympic Games) and the near contemporary (Charlotte Corday, guillotined in 1793 for assassinating the Jacobin Jean-Paul Marat), by way of myth (Amazon warrior Egée/Aegea). 'I have at heart', Hays wrote, 'the happiness of my sex, and their advancement in the grand scale of rational and social existence.'[4] As with Bell and Grant's plates, there is no suggestion that women can be funnelled into a single, totalizing category; in both cases, selection and arrangement invite unexpected conjunctions.

Austen was long believed deaf to the turmoil of the world. In the words of one twentieth-century male critic: 'Miss Austen composes novels almost extraterritorial to history.'[5] Conscripted to serve an idealized narrative of English identity, how could her domestic designs, those sedate village picnics and supper parties, imply any wider understanding or critique? Keen admirers of Austen's vision, the Bloomsbury artists reconceived history at the dinner table. Among Austen's best critics, Woolf recreated the novel as a way of countering women's dispossession through alternative, domestic histories intimately connected to the recognized public kind. She found in Austen something altogether revolutionary: 'a likeness to life'.[6]

In the later twentieth century, Bell and Grant's plates were thought lost, their only surviving witness the test plates and preliminary sketches and letters that passed between Bell and Jane Clark. Rediscovered, they returned to Charleston in 2018 thanks to grants from the Heritage Lottery Memorial Fund, the Art Fund and donations from 'a circle of remarkable women who each sponsored a plate'.[7]

37

Rex Whistler's costume designs for *Pride and Prejudice*, 1936

Despite her acknowledged reliance on techniques imported from the theatre—dramatic entrances and exits, set-piece encounters, vivid dialogue, strong characters—professional theatrical productions of Austen's novels got off to a slow start in comparison with those of her contemporary Walter Scott. His tartan-clad heroes took to the stage in the 1810s, her drawing-room heroines only around 1900, *Pride and Prejudice* quickly becoming a favourite with adapters.

Among the earliest, *Pride and Prejudice: A Sentimental Comedy in Three Acts* provides a glimpse into stage and screen glamour between the wars. Written by Australian Helen Jerome, the play opened to critical acclaim on Broadway in 1935 before transferring the following year to St James's Theatre in London's West End

where it enjoyed a 317-performance run.[1] Jerome's Mr Darcy is credited with releasing the potential of the buttoned-up figure of Austen's novel—a creation who would, after MGM optioned Jerome's play, rival Elizabeth Bennet for big-screen attention. With screenplay by the unlikely partnership of Aldous Huxley, whose dystopian fiction *Brave New World* had appeared in 1932, and leading Hollywood writer Jane Murfin, MGM's *Pride and Prejudice* (1940) starred Laurence Olivier, fresh from playing Heathcliff in *Wuthering Heights* (1939) and Maxim de Winter in *Rebecca* (1940). How could Elizabeth Bennet resist?

Meanwhile, in London Jerome's play had a new cast with new set and costume designs by fashionable society and commercial artist Rex Whistler.[2] In his short career, Whistler built a reputation for aristocratic commissions, striking domestic murals, celebrity portraits and elegant stage designs. With Nancy Mitford, Cecil Beaton and Edith Sitwell, he was one of the 'Bright Young Things', the Bohemian set of the interwar years. His costume designs include *The Tempest* (Shakespeare Memorial Theatre, Stratford, 1934–5) and *The Marriage of Figaro* (Sadler's Wells Theatre, London, 1934–5).

Six of his pen and watercolour sketches for the 1936 *Pride and Prejudice* are now in the Jane Austen's House collection: costume designs for Mrs Bennet, Lydia and Elizabeth Bennet, Mrs Gardiner and two for Lady Catherine de Bourgh. If, four years later, Hollywood's flamboyant antebellum-styled production encouraged female filmgoers to drool alongside Elizabeth Bennet (Greer Garson) over Olivier's Darcy, with Whistler's playful designs we are on different ground—a faint echo of the witty and slightly

fantastical revived baroque style of his murals. Lady Catherine, in purple braided pelisse with matching gloves and high plumed bonnet, the outfit she wears on stage to visit Elizabeth at Longbourn and warn her off marrying Mr Darcy, is an exaggerated figure—'in quotation marks', as Susan Sontag later defined 'camp' style.[3]

At St James's Theatre, in costumes executed to Whistler's designs by B.J. Simmons & Co. of Covent Garden, the new British cast featured, as Elizabeth Bennet, Celia Johnson, a rising star best remembered for the film *Brief Encounter* (1945), and, as Mr Darcy, the popular film actor Hugh Williams, who played James Steerforth in MGM's 1935 *David Copperfield*, the first sound production. Lady Catherine was the veteran stage and film actress Eva Moore.[4] Moore had been active in the women's suffrage movement and a founder in 1908 of the Actresses' Franchise League. During the First World War, while acting in the evenings, she served by day in the Women's Emergency Corps. A redoubtable woman and, you might think, a worthy Lady Catherine. By a curious twist of which Lady Catherine herself would surely have approved, she was also Laurence Olivier's real-life mother-in-law. As all readers of *Pride and Prejudice* might predict, the marriage was not a success.

Whistler was killed in Normandy in 1944, aged only thirty-nine, while serving with the Welsh Guards. Mrs G. Hartz of Bernardsville, New Jersey, gifted the six sketches to Jane Austen's House in 1995.[5]

38

Mr Darcy's shirt

The detective writer P.D. James described her beloved Jane
Austen's novels as 'Mills & Boon written by a genius'. Not so
long ago this would have seemed an odd remark. But that
was before Mr Darcy had a makeover.

Early BBC adaptations for television, beginning with *Pride
and Prejudice* in 1938, carried over techniques from stage and
radio: theatrical dialogue, artificial indoor sets, almost no
outdoor action.[1] Cameras were fixed and shots dominated by
close-ups of talking heads. Throughout the 1950s and 1960s,
a consciously imposed aesthetic distance signalled high
literature, parcelled up as teatime instruction for an audience
composed largely of children reading Austen for the school
syllabus. When on 18 December 1975 BBC One's *Omnibus*
presented a bicentenary programme, *Celebrating Jane Austen*,
with insightful renditions of Mrs Bennet and Miss Bates by
Celia Johnson (Elizabeth Bennet on stage in 1936), three
critics—American Mary McCarthy, Australian Germaine

Greer and Greek Arianna Stassinopoulos—invited to share their views described a novelist scarcely recognizable through today's democratic film-fashioned lens. To all three she appeared a deeply serious, moral writer using irony and manipulation of tone to set critical distance between her readers and characters. McCarthy offered sardonic comment on the superiority felt by those who belonged to the Jane Cult.

The 1980 BBC mini-series *Pride and Prejudice,* with screenplay by the feminist novelist Fay Weldon, marked the emergence of something new: moving camera shots, quick cuts, outdoor locations. Even so, viewers were not prepared for what burst onto their Sunday evening television screens between 24 September and 29 October 1995, when Mr Darcy cast off his outer clothing and emerged shirt dripping from the lake at Pemberley. Airing in the fourth episode of Andrew Davies's mini-series, that lake scene became an immediate sensation. Ten million viewers watched the sixth and final episode. Television classic adaptation was reinvented.

Mr Darcy now had a body: he fenced, boxed, swam and, yes, he stripped off. Our recent reinterpretation of Austenian romance owes much to the shift film marked from the novel's visual thrift and focus on the heroine's moral growth to the screen's sensual excesses and the hero's physical and emotional expressiveness. The prize—big house (aka 'money') and sex—this was a 1990s' fantasy. The lake scene encapsulates film's property in text.[2] Film has its own rhythm, less a matter of speaking to or about the origin text as breaking through to tell the story as if for the first time—escaping as well as honouring its source. This is why it was important that in 1995 Mr Darcy took a dip and that we do not look to find it in the book—though how many readers have?

Then there's that shirt, designed by Dinah Collin from an antique original. The Regency linen shirt was underwear, an intimate garment worn next to the skin, pulled on and off over the head, only its collar and cuffs intended for public display. With its Byronic coding the shirt signalled more than costume makeover; it restyled the austere Austen hero as athletic and sexy. Wet, the shirt clung to the body. This is Jane Austen's world filtered through Charlotte or Emily Brontë's—exposed to nature and smouldering tastefully.

Like a medieval relic, the Darcy shirt toured Britain during the BBC centenary celebrations of 2022 as one of the '100 Objects that made the BBC'.[3] But, like other relics, it's not as unique as you might think: six identical shirts were used in the production. Colin Firth, playing Mr Darcy, had a stunt double; the underwater segment of the scene was filmed in a tank at Ealing Studios, West London. Wet shirts, dry shirts and shirts spray-misted to appear damp as Mr Darcy strode away from the undipped-in lake were all needed.

39

A tea caddy

'At 9 o'clock she made breakfast—*that* was *her* part of
the household work—The tea and sugar stores were
under *her* charge—*and* the wine.'[1]

Tea is mentioned in 37 of Austen's 161 surviving letters;
coffee in 8. Tea is drunk in every one of her novels,
often by invitation and several hours after dinner. In
fashionable circles, dinner was eaten late, hence also
later teas. Austen uses appointed hours as subtle social
markers: at countrified Steventon on 18 December 1798
the family dined 'at half after Three' and drank tea
'at half after six'. 'I am afraid you will despise us', she
wrote to Cassandra, on a visit to elegant Godmersham
Park.[2] Steventon ways are surely remembered in the
three o'clock dinners followed by early tea at Stanton
Rectory in *The Watsons*, viewed with mock-horror by
the zealously fashionable Tom Musgrave, who never
dines before 8 p.m.[3] In Austen's novels tea drinking,

a more intimate affair than dinner, is the occasion for conversation, revelation and speculation. Fast-forward to our own times: in reality-television series *RuPaul's Drag Race* (airing in the UK since 2009), '(spilling the) tea' is slang for 'gossip'.

Imported from China and India, tea was expensive, kept under lock and key. With tea comes sugar. The consumption of both was increasing as Georgian England adjusted to a new era in its imperial venturing. Sugar, the product of slavery, was political. Protective duties on West Indian sugar gave plantation owners virtual monopoly over the British market. Her letters show Austen keenly aware of sugar's fluctuating price and the need to ration supplies, but with no evidence that, unlike those gentry women dubbed 'anti-saccharites', she boycotted sugar within the home.

There is, however, *Mansfield Park*, interpreted since the 1980s in an abolitionist context.[4] Much hangs on a single sentence, Fanny Price's question to her uncle, Sir Thomas Bertram, newly returned from his Antiguan estates: 'Did not you hear me ask him about the slave trade last night?' (ch. 21). The novel, published in 1814, takes as its subject the moral reform of the Bertrams. Britain had banned the trade (though not slavery itself) only in 1807. Hints pile up: the title's apparent allusion to the famous 'Mansfield Judgement' of 1772 that no slave could be forcibly removed from England and sold back into slavery; Fanny's enjoyment of abolitionist poet William Cowper; cruel Aunt Norris, Fanny's tormentor, named after the former 'slave-captain' in Thomas Clarkson's *History of ... the Abolition of Slavery* (1808), an author Austen references admiringly as she writes the novel.[5]

Is the reader invited to compare Fanny's oppressed state, a servant at Lady Bertram's tea table, with slavery? Or is this too inappropriate a connection? And how to understand her question?

If the novel's narrative is contemporary with its writing, hers is a post-abolition enquiry, though as a plantation owner her uncle's wealth (and her own comfort) would remain indebted to slave labour. Then there's the situation of his plantation: Antigua, one of the oldest of the British West Indian colonies. Antigua's planters had much to gain by supporting abolition: their land was exhausted and returns falling. On naval duty in the West Indies in 1805–6, Austen's brother Frank formed a hostile impression of the treatment of slaves. On the other hand, he profited handsomely from Britain's imperial expansion in India and China, which found other means to exploit distant peoples and resources.[6] Conflicted and complicit, the novel now appears a vehicle for complex cultural anxieties.

This is Jane Austen's tea caddy, donated to Jane Austen's House in 1972 by a descendant of James Goodchild, brother-in-law to William Littleworth (see Object 19), who began working for the Austens in July 1816 and continued until Cassandra died in 1845. And, finally, Jane Austen ordered the family tea from Twinings at 216 The Strand, London, where it still stands.

40

Grayson Perry, 'Jane Austen in E17', 2009

E17 is the postcode of Walthamstow. Grayson Perry's pot contrasts middle-class polite culture with the world of North-east London council houses. He invites us to reconsider Elizabeth Jenkins's mock-horrified response to the 'new gas fire glittering like a set of fake teeth' usurping the place of the old grate in Chawton Cottage (see Object 29). Sixty years on, Perry flips things the other way. Where Jenkins shuddered at the vulgar defacement of a hallowed spot, Perry relishes the potential of his signature guerrilla tactics to ambush the unsuspecting art lover. Jenkins's vision of civilization restored is matched by Perry's representation of civilization exposed. The class-bound contours of taste are his regular subject matter. In 2003 he won the prestigious British Turner Prize with pots whose manufacture and form were in stark contrast to the disturbing images (child abuse, for example) that decorated them. Now he turned his gaze to that national treasure and darling of the establishment, Jane Austen.

Perry's ceramic pot is a joyful object that explodes with colour and sensual delight. Richly incised with brightly painted, stylized images of genteel ladies in Regency costume, drinking tea, it appears a gentle parody of the polite drawing rooms and calm, ordered lives of Jane Austen's English villages. But look closer: those tea-drinking ladies are juxtaposed with layered photographic transfers, adverts, snippets from celebrity gossip magazines and sites around Perry's studio in E17. Would Austen have been startled to see her social world reduced to kitsch? What does the pot say about divisions in Britain in the opening decade of the twenty-first century?

Perry's art is about contrast. He regularly draws inspiration from high culture and street culture, mixing and holding the two in tension. The pot is exquisitely beautiful in design. Its classical shape was made using the basic, time-consuming coil method (rather than casting or throwing) to build up the clay in layers. Classical form, with its intimations of antiquity, challenges the view that, in the art hierarchy, the potter's skill is no more than decorative craft. At the same time, Austen's classic novels, made over, absorbed and amplified from the mid-1990s into the lavish visual imagery of the heritage film industry, are here set against the far different inheritance of a post-industrial society. A less comfortable vision emerges between and beneath the embossed and brightly glazed bonnets, parasols and tea tables on the pot's surface. Exaggerated baby heads are interspersed with warning notices: 'Look out'; 'THIS AREA

IS UNDER 24 HOUR TV SURVEILLANCE. TRESPASSERS WILL BE PROSECUTED'; the message 'JESUS IS ALIVE' above three crosses.

In a nice coincidence, Austen assumed her eminent position in the movie business in the same year, 1995, that the National Trust celebrated its centenary. A decade on, with Britain in the grip of economic recession, Perry's satiric vision set fat-cat enclaves and country estates against urban blight and council estates, two sides of the heritage coin. The eye is not permitted to settle in a single register but shifts between contrasting popular packaging of cultural codes. 'I want to make something that lives with the eye as a beautiful piece of art, but on closer inspection, a polemic or an ideology will come out of it.'[1]

Whose England does Jane Austen now represent? What social divisions does heritage nostalgia distract us from or blind us to? Depending on your view, the pot's message is playful or hints at something darker and more fragile in social relations.

Glazed ceramic, the pot stands 100 × 51.5 cm (39¾ × 20¼ inches). It is in the collection of Manchester City Art Gallery.

41

Last words

From a life lived with pen in hand, this may be the most poign-
ant object to survive: the last page of the novel Jane Austen left
unfinished in manuscript at her death. Now called *Sanditon*,
a title attributed by her niece Anna Lefroy, it was long known
simply as 'The Last Work', though, according to family tradition,
Austen's working title for it was 'The Brothers'.[1] A single thread
of words, suspended in empty space, they read 'fire constantly
occupied by Sir H.D.' followed by the date 'March 18'. She died
exactly four months later. The page lies mid-way through the
handmade booklet, the third of three into which she had so far
written twelve chapters of her new novel. Behind it lie thirty-nine
filled pages; ahead are forty blanks.

As a writer, she was better at beginnings than endings, though
her comic deathbed verses on the subject of Winchester races,
composed 15 July 1817, possess a defiant panache.[2] Here, at least,
she finished with a flourish. Unlike *Sanditon*, there is no known

fire constantly occupied by Sir H. D.

March 18.

manuscript of the poem in her hand. And with the evidence of the hand we have something that affects us differently.

This word thread is not just the final sentence of an unfinished novel, a few words that attach to and round off the narrative so far. The frame of the otherwise blank page refocuses attention from one kind of meaning to another: from linguistic to visual signs. Within its frame, and estranged from the rest of the text, their form becomes significant—the shape of the letters, the spaces between, their position and appearance on the page and the physical act they connote. We stare hard and imagine they might mediate an essential identity—what was in her mind as she signed them off, unfinished? Did she expect to return the next day or next week? Or did she know what we know? Five days later, on 23 March 1817, she wrote to her niece Fanny Knight, 'about a week ago I was very poorly ... Sickness is a dangerous Indulgence at my time of Life.'[3] In the frame of the page, transposed here into the frame of a photograph, words are open to endless speculation; they possess new properties: how they look affects how they mean, and they provoke an emotional response. The question is not what do we read, but how do we feel when we look?

Unfinished works are not easily detached from their point of origin; author biography plays a special part in how we make sense of them. Or, turned around, they might as easily stand in for, become a credible illusion of, the interrupted life, ended mid-way, its own last forty pages blank. 'Space does not exist', wrote the French-American artist Louise Bourgeois. 'It is just a metaphor for the structure of our existence.'[4] So much of the structure Austen's life has assumed has taken shape after her early death. Like this slender thread of words, she too has become an artefact, shaped and reshaped in our subsequent imaginings—in what we have written across her blank page. Hers will always be an unfinished portrait.

The holograph manuscript of Jane Austen's final novel, written between 27 January and 18 March 1817, was presented by her great-great-niece, Mary Isabella Lefroy, to King's College, Cambridge, in 1930, in memory of her sister, Florence Emma, and brother-in-law, Augustus Austen-Leigh, provost of King's, and his wife. Both were Austen family descendants, Augustus the son of Austen's family biographer James Edward.

Notes

ABBREVIATIONS

The following abbreviated titles are used:

Lady Susan   Jane Austen, *Lady Susan, The Watsons, and Sanditon*, ed. Kathryn Sutherland, Oxford University Press, Oxford, 2021.

Letters   *Jane Austen's Letters*, ed. Deirdre Le Faye, 4th edn, Oxford University Press, Oxford, 2011.

Family Record   Deirdre Le Faye, *Jane Austen: A Family Record*, 2nd edn, Cambridge University Press, Cambridge, 2004.

Memoir   *A Memoir of Jane Austen and Other Family Recollections*, ed. Kathryn Sutherland, Oxford University Press, Oxford, 2002.

Teenage Writings   Jane Austen, *Teenage Writings*, ed. Kathryn Sutherland and Freya Johnston, Oxford University Press, Oxford, 2017.

References to Austen's novels follow the practice of modern editions citing passages by continuous chapter numbers, not by volume and chapter number. References to Austen's letters are also given by date written, to allow readers to discover them in any edition.

INTRODUCTION

1. Comparison might be made with the objects itemized in Cassandra Austen's testamentary letter, disposing of her effects after death: mainly clothing and jewellery, they were passed on to female relations or female servants. The letter is reproduced in *Jane Austen's Fiction Manuscripts*, ed. Kathryn Sutherland, 5 vols, Oxford University Press, Oxford, 2018, vol. 5, pp. 300–307.
2. *Memoir*, p. 14; *Family Record*, p. 20.

3. Robin Vick, 'The Sale at Steventon Parsonage', *Jane Austen Society, Collected Reports*, 1986–95, pp. 295–8.

4. *Letters*, p. 88.

5. *Letters*, p. 355. Though legally invalid (it was unwitnessed), the will was nevertheless officially proved on 10 September 1817. For details of its provision, see *Family Record*, p. 259, and J.G., 'A Jane Austen Document from Somerset House', *Jane Austen Society, Collected Reports*, 1966–75, pp. 38–9. Cassandra Austen sold her five copyrights (that of *Pride and Prejudice* had been sold in 1812) to the publisher Richard Bentley in 1832. See Kathryn Sutherland, 'Jane Austen's Dealings with John Murray and His Firm', *Review of English Studies* 64, 2012, pp. 105–26, at pp. 115–16 and n.38.

6. *Family Record*, pp. 153, 163.

7. Jan Fergus, *Jane Austen, A Literary Life*, Macmillan, London, 1991, pp. 190–91 n.47; Tony Corley, 'Jane Austen's Dealings with Her Publishers', *Jane Austen Society, Report*, 2011, pp. 127–38, at pp. 130–31.

8. *Letters*, p. 33.

9. Deirdre le Faye, *A Chronology of Jane Austen and her Family*, Cambridge University Press, Cambridge, 2006, p. 223.

10. 'Women and Fiction' (1929), in Virginia Woolf, *Women and Writing*, ed. Michèle Barrett, The Women's Press, London, 1979, pp. 44, 49–50.

11. Deborah Kaplan, *Jane Austen among Women*, Johns Hopkins University Press, Baltimore MD and London, 1992, p. 41.

12. *Teenage Writings*, pp. 64, 47, 30.

13. *Letters*, p. 142.

14. Barbara Hardy, *A Reading of Jane Austen*, repr. Athlone Press, London, 1979 (1975), pp. 160–65.

15. *Letters*, p. 186.

16. *Letters*, p. 78. See also p. 123: 'My expectation of having nothing to say to you after the conclusion of my last, seems nearer the Truth than I thought it would be'; 8 February 1807.

17. *Letters*, p. 234 (23 February 1813).

18. *Letters*, p. 133 (17 June 1808).

19. Carol Houlihan Flynn, 'The Letters', in Edward Copeland and Juliet McMaster (eds), *The Cambridge Companion to Jane Austen*, Cambridge University Press, Cambridge, 2011, pp. 97–110, at p. 108.

20. *Letters*, p. 297.

21. These items all appear in *The Morning Chronicle*, 24 December 1810, a newspaper we know the Austens read.

22. Dorothy Van Ghent, *The English Novel: Form and Function*, Harper & Brothers, New York, 1953, pp. 110–11.

23. *Letters*, p. 145 (1 October 1808); p. 159 (25 October 1808); p. 206 (24 January 1813).

24. *Letters*, pp. 261, 266, 283.
25. Diana Fuss, *The Sense of an Interior: Four Writers and the Rooms that Shaped Them*, Routledge, New York and London, 2004, p. 4.
26. *Memoir*, pp. 81–2.
27. *Memoir*, p. 173.
28. Edward W. Said, *Culture and Imperialism*, Chatto & Windus, London, 1993, pp. 100–101, cited in Bharat Tandon, *Jane Austen and the Morality of Conversation*, Anthem Press, London, 2003, p. 195.
29. *Letters*, p. 53.
30. *Memoir*, pp. 82, 116.
31. Arjun Appadurai, 'Commodities and the Politics of Value', in Appadurai (ed.), *The Social Life of Things: Commodities in Cultural Perspective*, Cambridge University Press, Cambridge, 1986, pp. 3–63, at p. 5.
32. Jane Bennett, *Vibrant Matter: A Political Ecology of Things*, Duke University Press, Durham NC, 2010, p. 6.
33. For 'it-narratives', see Mark Blackwell (ed.), *The Secret Life of Things*, Bucknell University Press, Lewisburg PA, 2007.
34. *Northanger Abbey*, ed. Marilyn Butler, Penguin, London, 2003 (1995), p. xxvi.
35. *Letters*, pp. 57, 340, 350, 26.
36. *The Life of Mary Russell Mitford*, vol. 1, ed. A.G.K. L'Estrange, London, 1870, pp. 305–6.
37. Adam Phillips, 'Against Biography', in *In Writing*, Penguin, London, 2019 (2016), pp. 43–63.
38. Appadurai, 'Commodities and the Politics of Value', p. 5.
39. Sylvia Plath, *The Journals of Sylvia Plath, 1950–62*, ed. Karen V. Kukil, Faber & Faber, London, 2000, pp. 588–9.
40. Nicola J. Watson, *The Author's Effects: On Writer's House Museums*, Oxford University Press, Oxford, 2020, p. 108.
41. Roland Barthes, *Sade/Fourier/Loyola*, trans. Richard Miller, Jonathan Cape, London, 1977 (1971), p. 9.
42. Italo Calvino, *Six Memos for the Next Millenium*, trans. Geoffrey Brock, Penguin, London, 2016 (1988), p. 151.

PORTRAIT OF JANE AUSTEN

1. 26 October 1932, Heinz Archive and Library, National Portrait Gallery, London, RWC/HH, unfoliated.
2. Anna Lefroy to James Edward Austen-Leigh, 20 July [1869], Heinz Archive and Library, National Portrait Gallery, London, RWC/HH, unfoliated.
3. See Richard Brilliant, *Portraiture*, Reaktion Books, London, 1991, p. 19.

MRS AUSTEN TO MRS WALTER

1. Laurence Sterne, *Tristram Shandy*, 1759–67, vol. 1, ch. 4.
2. *Austen Papers, 1704–1856*, ed. R. A. Austen-Leigh, Spottiswoode, Ballantyne & Co., London, 1942, p. 31.
3. Ibid., pp. 32–3.
4. *Letters*, p. 130 (15 June 1808).
5. *Letters*, p. 190 (25 April 1811); p. 210 (29 January 1813); p. 323 (?December 1815).
6. *Memoir*, p. 43.
7. *Letters*, p. 103 (8 April 1805).
8. Henry James, 'The Art of Fiction' (1884), *The Portable Henry James*, ed. Morton Dauwen Zabel, Penguin, Harmondsworth, 1977, p. 397. James is described as Austen's 'one son' in Rudyard Kipling, 'The Janeites', *Debits and Credits*, Macmillan, London, 1926, pp. 153–4.

THE REVD GEORGE AUSTEN'S BOOKCASE

1. *Letters*, p. 77 (14 January 1801). See also David Gilson, 'Jane Austen's Books', *Book Collector* 23, 1974, pp. 27–39.
2. Karen Thomson, 'Mrs Musgrave of Newton Priors? Jane Austen and Sir Isaac Newton's Library', *Persuasions On-line*, vol. 38, no. 1, 2017, www.jasna. org.
3. *Teenage Writings*, pp. 84–5.
4. *Letters*, p. 124.

'VOLUME THE FIRST'

1. Emily Brontë, *Wuthering Heights*, 1847, ch. 12.
2. See 'Henry and Eliza' and 'The beautifull Cassandra', in *Teenage Writings*, pp. 27–32, 37–40.
3. Virginia Woolf, 'Jane Austen Practising', *New Statesman*, 15 July 1922, her review of *Love & Freindship and Other Early Works, now first printed from the original ms. by Jane Austen*, preface by G.K. Chesterton, Chatto & Windus, London, 1922.

MARIANNE KNIGHT'S DANCING SLIPPERS

1. 'A Tour through Wales', in *Teenage Writings*, p. 156.
2. Susan Mein Sibbald (1783–1812), *The Memoirs of Susan Sibbald*, ed. Francis Paget Hett, John Lane, London, 1926, p. 248.
3. *Memoir*, p. 139.
4. Thomas Brown (pseud. for Tom Moore), *Intercepted Letters; or, The Twopenny Post-Bag*, J. Carr, London, 1813, p. 40.

MARRIAGE REGISTER, ST NICHOLAS CHURCH

1. *Family Record*, p. 70, dates the entries conjecturally to 1790, when Jane Austen was fourteen.
2. The act came into force in April 1754, requiring a separate register to be kept for marriages and a set form of words to be used, often, as here in the Steventon register, supplied in printed form. Entries had to be signed by both parties to the marriage and by at least two witnesses. At this time, the only exceptions to parish church marriage were for Quakers and Jews.
3. *Teenage Writings*, pp. 3, 5, 26, 55, 14, 206 (in a late addition to the tale made by the teenage James Edward Austen).
4. In 1799 and 1801 she acted more officially, in the temporary capacity of her father's clerk, writing up entries of baptism and burial in the parish registers (*Family Record*, pp. 110, 131).

BETSY HANCOCK/ELIZA DE FEUILLIDE

1. Deirdre Le Faye, *Jane Austen's 'Outlandish Cousin': The Life and Letters of Eliza de Feuillide*, British Library, London, 2002, p. 54.
2. Ibid., p. 103.
3. Charlotte and Gwendolen Mitchell, 'Passages to India: Did Joshua Reynolds Paint a Portrait of Jane Austen's Aunt?', *Times Literary Supplement*, 21 July 2017, pp. 13–14.

JANE AUSTEN'S MUSIC BOOK

1. *Letters*, p. 168.
2. *Memoir*, p. 170.
3. *Memoir*, p. 194.
4. This music book and others from the collection at Jane Austen's House are available as digital facsimiles in *The Austen Family Music Books*, https://archive.org/details/austenfamilymusicbooks. See Jeanice Brooks, 'In Search of Austen's Missing Songs', *Review of English Studies* 67, November 2016, pp. 914–45.

MUSLIN SHAWL

1. Hilary Davidson, *Dress in the Age of Jane Austen: Regency Fashion*, Yale University Press, New Haven CT and London, 2019, pp. 269–74.
2. *Letters*, p. 31 (25 December 1798); p. 267 (2 March 1814).
3. *Teenage Writings*, p. 5.
4. Park Honan, *Jane Austen: Her Life*, Fawcett Columbine, New York, 1987, p. 69, highlights the 'shady' aspects of some of Frank's oriental work. See also Brian Southam, *Jane Austen and the Navy*, Hambledon, London, 2000, pp. 97–8; and Clive Caplan, 'The Ships of Frank Austen', Jane Austen Society, *Report*, 2008, pp. 74–86, at pp. 80–81.

5. For a passage to India as the fate of Mary Wynne in 'Kitty, or the Bower, see *Teenage Writings*, p. 170. *Martha Lloyd's Household Book*, ed. Julienne Gehrer, Bodleian Library Publishing, Oxford, 2021, contains several recipes for curry, at pp. 92, 99, 113.

THE TRIAL OF MRS LEIGH PERROT

1. Mrs Leigh Perrot writing to her cousin Mountague Cholmeley, 10 October 1799, *Austen Papers*, p. 195.
2. From the transcript of the testimony of the Revd Mr Wake, Curate of St Michael's, Bath, in *Trial of Mrs. Leigh Perrot*, 2nd edn, Printed in London by J.W. Myers, No. 2, Paternoster-Row; and C. Chapple, No. 66, Pall-Mall, 1800, p. 25 (Jane Austen's House copy).
3. For example, 'An Account of the Trial of Mrs. Leigh Perrot', *Lady's Magazine*, London, April 1800, printed with an engraved portrait.
4. Deirdre Le Faye, 'Another Piece of Missing Lace', Jane Austen Society, *Report*, 2003, pp. 31–2, notes a similar incident, this time in Scarborough, North Yorkshire, recorded by Susan Sibbald in her *Memoirs* (see Object 5).
5. *Letters*, p. 89.
6. Sarah Markham, 'A Gardener's Question for Mrs Leigh Perrot', Jane Austen Society, *Collected Reports*, 1986–95, pp. 213–14.
7. In W. and R.A. Austen-Leigh, *Jane Austen, Her Life and Letters*, Smith, Elder, & Co., London, 1913, p. 135. See also Sir Frank Douglas MacKinnon, *Grand Larceny*, Oxford University Press, London, 1937, by a celebrated high- court judge and avowed Janeite, and David Pugsley, 'The Trial of Jane Austen's Aunt Jane Leigh Perrot and the Opinion of John Morris, KC', *Persuasions On-line*, vol. 41, no. 1, 2020, www.jasna.org.

SILHOUETTE OF CASSANDRA

1. *Austen Papers*, pp. 32–3.
2. *Memoir*, p. 160.
3. *Letters*, p. 260 (13 November 1813).
4. *Letters*, pp. 359–60 (20 July 1817).
5. *Memoir*, p. 187.
6. Claire Tomalin, *Jane Austen: A Life*, Viking, London, 1997, p. 195.
7. The name for these outline portraits derives from that of Étienne de Silhouette (1709–1767), a French author and politician, and with two possible explanations: either it was intended to ridicule Silhouette's petty economies when French Controller-general, or in acknowledgement of his making of such portraits to adorn the walls of his château. 'silhouette, n., Etymology'. *Oxford English Dictionary*, Oxford University Press, July 2023, https://doi.org/10.1093/OED/2726284555.
8. William Henry Fox Talbot, *Some Account of the Art of Photogenic Drawing*, R. & J.E. Taylor, London, 1839.

A FLOWER SPRAY

1. 'Jane Austen House for the Nation', *Hull Daily Mail*, 20 July 1949, p. 3; 'Austen "Scraps" Wanted', *Evening News and Southern Daily Mail*, 10 July 1950; 'Relics', Jane Austen Society, *Collected Reports*, 1949–65, pp. 22–3.
2. *Letters*, p. 44.
3. *Letters*, pp. 46–7.

FRANCES BURNEY, *CAMILLA*

1. Kathryn Sutherland, 'Jane Austen's Dealings with John Murray and His Firm', *Review of English Studies* 64, 2012, pp. 105–26, at pp. 113–14.
2. *Letters*, p. 138 (26 June 1808).
3. The list has been described as 'arguably the most famous in literary history, certainly in the history of the novel', P.D. Garside, 'Jane Austen and Subscription History', *British Journal of the Eighteenth Century* 10, 1987, pp. 175–88, at p. 175. See also Joceyln Harris, 'Jane Austen and the Subscription List to *Camilla* (1796)', *Persuasions On-line*, vol. 35, no. 1, 2004, www.jasna.org.
4. *Memoir*, p. 105.
5. *Roland Barthes by Roland Barthes*, trans. Richard Howard, Vintage, London, 2020 (1975), p. 51.
6. John Feltham, *A Guide to All the Watering and Sea-Bathing Places*, new edn, London, 1815, p. 113.
7. *Letters*, p. 279 (10 August 1814).
8. *Letters*, p. 27 (18 December 1798); pp. 207–8 (24 January 1813). See Robin Vick, 'The Alton Book Society', Jane Austen Society, *Collected Reports*, 1986–95, pp. 353–5.
9. *Letters*, p. 310 (23 November 1815).
10. The pencilled insertion, in Jane Austen's hand, reads: 'Since this work went to the Press, a circumstance of some Importance to the happiness of Camilla has taken place, namely that Dr Marchmont has at last'... A remark to Cassandra, 5 September 1796, may suggest the insertion was made around that time: 'Give my Love to Mary Harrison, & tell her I wish whenever she is attached to a young Man, some respectable Dr Marchmont may keep them apart for five Volumes', *Letters*, p. 9. Austen's copy of *Camilla*, one of the few books we can be sure she owned, was presented to the Bodleian Library in 1930 by Captain Ernest Austen, R.N., grandson of Jane's brother Frank. See R.W. Chapman, 'Jane Austen's *Camilla*', *Bodleian Quarterly Record* 6, 1930, pp. 162–3. For books Jane Austen owned, see Object 3, n.1.

A LETTER

1. *Letters*, p. 94.
2. *Letters*, p. 186 (18 April 1811).

3. Ann Spokes Symonds, 'The Beecher Hogans and the Austen Crosses', Jane Austen Society, *Report*, 2004, pp. 30–34.

PORTRAIT OF JANE AUSTEN

1. Sir Egerton Brydges, brother to the young Jane Austen's mentor Anne Lefroy, recalled in later life that she was 'fair and handsome, slight and elegant, but with cheeks a little too full', in *Memoir*, p. 44.
2. Thomas Smith, *The Young Artist's Assistant in the Art of Drawing in Water Colours*, Sherwood, Gilbert & Piper, London, 1824, lists the twelve colours considered most suitable for the amateur as Indigo, Prussian Blue (deep blue), Venetian Red (inclining to scarlet), Yellow Ochre, Gamboge (mustard yellow), Raw Umber (yellowish brown), Vandyke Brown (deep brown), Burnt Sienna (brown), Burnt Umber (reddish brown), Sepia and Lamp Black. See Susan Owens, 'A Life in Portraits', in Kathryn Sutherland (ed.), *Jane Austen, Writer in the World*, Bodleian Library Publishing, Oxford, 2017, pp. 164–85.
3. Anna Lefroy to James Edward Austen-Leigh, 8 August [1862], Hampshire Record Office, Winchester, Austen-Leigh Archive, MS. 23M93/86/3c. 118 (iii), 2v.
4. 20 July [1869], Heinz Archive and Library, National Portrait Gallery, London, RWC/HH, unfoliated.

WALLPAPER FRAGMENT

1. Anna Lefroy from the Lefroy Manuscript, a family history, quoted in *Family Record*, p. 73.
2. The detail is recorded in the ledger of the Basingstoke furnisher John Ring; see entry for 2 March 1795, in Deirdre Le Faye, *A Chronology of Jane Austen and her Family*, Cambridge University Press, Cambridge, 2006, p. 173.
3. John Lukacs, 'The Bourgeois Interior', *The American Scholar*, vol. 34, no. 4, 1970, pp. 616–30, at p. 623.
4. Virginia Woolf, *A Room of One's Own*, Penguin, Harmondsworth, 1973 (1928), pp. 74, 87.
5. *Letters*, p. 57 (8 November 1800); p. 340 (23 January 1817); p. 350 (14 March 1817).
6. *Teenage Writings*, pp. 169–70.

MARTHA LLOYD'S HOUSEHOLD BOOK

1. *Letters*, p. 21.
2. *Letters*, p. 20 (17 November 1798); p. 114 (27 August 1805); p. 303 (17 October 1815); p. 337 (17 December 1816).
3. *Letters*, p. 200 (31 May 1811).
4. *Letters*, p. 144.

5. *Teenage Writings*, p. 11.
6. *Teenage Writings*, pp. 98–100.
7. For a full facsimile, see *Martha Lloyd's Household Book*, ed. Julienne Gehrer, Bodleian Library Publishing, Oxford, 2021.

AUSTEN FAMILY QUILT

1. *Memoir*, pp. 171, 173.
2. *Letters*, p. 199.
3. *Letters*, p. 337 (16 December 1816).
4. *The Letters of Samuel Beckett*, Volume 1: *1929–40*, ed. Martha Dow Fehsenfeld and Lois More Overbeck, Cambridge University Press, Cambridge, 2009, p. 250.
5. See Lucy Bailey, Elizabeth Betts and Sue Dell (eds), *Stories in Stitches: Reimagining Jane Austen's Quilt*, Jane Austen's House Publications, Chawton, 2018.

JANE AUSTEN'S WRITING TABLE

1. *Letters*, p. 15.
2. *Letters*, p. 124 (8 February 1807).
3. Gaston Bachelard, *The Poetics of Space*, trans. Maria Jolas, Beacon Press, Boston MA, 1994 (1958), p. 78.
4. William Littleworth (1795–1878). The Littleworths (also known as Littlewart) served the Austens over several generations. John and Elizabeth were foster parents for Mrs Austen's babies; their daughter-in-law, Nanny, was Jane's hairdresser; Jane became godmother to one of Nanny's daughters. See Deirdre Le Faye, 'The Austens and the Littleworths', Jane Austen Society, *Collected Reports*, 1986–95, pp. 64–70.

FOUR WEDGWOOD DISHES

1. Deidre Shauna Lynch, 'Counter Publics: Shopping and Women's Sociability', in Gillian Russell and Clara Tuite (eds), *Romantic Sociability: Social Networks and Literary Culture in Britain, 1770–1840*, Cambridge University Press, Cambridge, 2002, pp. 211–36; and Irene Collins, 'Jane Austen and the Art of "Polite Shopping"', Jane Austen Society, *Report*, 2011, pp. 139–41.
2. *Letters*, p. 202.

THEATRE BILL, COVENT GARDEN

1. *Letters*, p. 228.
2. See Paula Byrne, *Jane Austen and the Theatre*, Hambledon, London, 2002.
3. *Letters*, p. 230 (16 September 1813).
4. *Letters*, p. 240 (25 September 1813).
5. *Teenage Writings*, p. 78.

6. For a description of the refurbished Theatre Royal, Covent Garden, see John Feltham, *The Picture of London for 1818*, Longman, Hurst, Rees, Orme, & Brown, London, 1818, pp. 288–92; and Edward Wedlake Brayley, *Historical and Descriptive Accounts of the Theatres of London*, J. Taylor, London, 1826, pp. 19–20.

FRONT DOOR, 50 ALBEMARLE STREET

1. Georg Simmel, 'Bridge and Door', in Neil Leach (ed.), *Rethinking Architecture: A Reader in Cultural Theory*, Routledge, London, 1997, p. 67.
2. *Letters*, pp. 307–8 (3 November 1815). The letter survives as pencil draft and as the version sent to Murray, with slight change in wording. The drafted words 'I must beg the favour of you to call on me' became in the version sent 'I must request the favour of you to call on me'.
3. *Memoir*, p. 150.
4. *The Letters of John Murray to Lord Byron*, ed. Andrew Nicholson, Liverpool University Press, Liverpool, 2007, p. 218.

EMMA, THE WINDSOR CASTLE COPY

1. *Letters*, p. 308 (15 November 1815).
2. *Letters*, p. 315.
3. *Letters*, pp. 216–17.
4. *Letters*, p. 287 (9 September 1814).
5. *Teenage Writings*, p. 23.
6. As Thomas Keymer puts it, the highest ranks are 'thinly represented' in her fictions and 'Austen's attitude to aristocratic manners is one of general neglect, punctuated by occasional disdain'; 'Rank', in Janet Todd (ed.), *Jane Austen in Context*, Cambridge University Press, Cambridge, 2005, pp. 387–96, at p. 389.
7. *Letters*, pp. 317, 318.
8. David Gilson, *A Bibliography of Jane Austen*, corrected edn, St Paul's Bibliographies, Winchester, 1997, A8, p. 69.

A LIFE IN BANKNOTES

1. W.H. Auden and Louis MacNeice, *Letters from Iceland*, Faber & Faber, London, 1967, p. 19.
2. £630 works out as a yearly income of £90, between 1811 and 1817, her publishing years—not enough to live on. Posthumous profits and Cassandra Austen's sale of her sister's remaining copyrights in 1832 brought Austen's overall earnings from her novels to around £1,625, most of which were received after death. See Jan Fergus, *Jane Austen, A Literary Life*, Macmillan, London, 1991, pp. 171, 193 n.90.
3. *Letters*, p. 135 (22 June 1808).
4. *Teenage Writings*, p. 96.

5. 'Kitty, or the Bower', in *Teenage Writings*, p. 178.
6. See Tony Corley, 'Jane Austen's Dealings with her Publishers', Jane Austen Society, *Report*, 2011, p. 134.

JANE AUSTEN'S PELISSE

1. *Letters*, p. 283. See Hilary Davidson, *Jane Austen's Wardrobe*, Yale University Press, New Haven CT and London, 2023, pp. 107–13.
2. In 2011, at her marriage to Prince William, the embroidery on the sleeves of Kate Middleton's wedding dress, designed by Sarah Burton, creative director at Alexander McQueen, incorporated the flowers of the four countries of the United Kingdom (English roses, Scottish thistles, Welsh daffodils and Irish shamrocks).
3. For example, *Letters*, pp. 149–51 (7 October 1808); p. 173 (17 January 1809); pp. 268–9 (5 March 1814); p. 285 (2 September 1814).

THE OCTAGON ROOM, BATH

1. David Gilson, 'Jane Austen's Books', *Book Collector* 23, 1974, pp. 27–39.
2. A contemporary account describes it as 'an octagon of 48 feet diameter, adorned with a portrait of Captain Wade, by Gainsborough', noting that 'Concerts are on Wednesday nights during the season' (John Feltham, *A Guide to All the Watering and Sea-Bathing Places*, new edn, London, 1815, p. 40).

THE DONKEY CARRIAGE

1. *Teenage Writings*, p. 36.
2. *Letters*, p. 282. Oscar Fay Adams, *The Story of Jane Austen's Life*, A.C. McClurg & Co., Chicago IL, 1891, p. 178.
3. See Janine Barchas, 'Jane and Taxes: the Duty-Free Donkey Trap', Jane Austen Society, *Report*, 2021, pp. 88–96.
4. *Memoir*, p. 177.
5. *Letters*, p. 337 (16 December 1816).
6. Letters, p. 348 (13 March 1817); p. 353 (26 March).
7. *Letters*, p. 341 (24 January 1817).

A LOCK OF HAIR

1. The letter, addressed to brother Charles and dated 9 May 1843 (MS. MA 7279, Morgan Library, New York), is transcribed in full in *Jane Austen's Fiction Manuscripts*, ed. Kathryn Sutherland, 5 vols, Oxford University Press, Oxford, 2018, vol. 5, pp. 300–307.
2. John Donne, 'The Relic', line 6.
3. André Maurois, *Byron*, trans. Hamish Miles, Jonathan Cape, London, 1930, p. 184, mentions the poet's hair trickery; adjusted in Fiona McCarthy, *Byron, Life and Legend*, John Murray, London, 2002, p. 194. On Byron's

theto of the hair of Lucretia Borgia, see Claudia Giuliani and Diego Saglia, 'Byron's Hair', in Romantic Europe: The Virtual Exhibition (RÊVE), posted 27 October 2017, www.euromanticism.org/virtual-exhibition.

4. *Memoir*, p. 169.
5. 'Jane Austen's Hair', Jane Austen Society, *Collected Reports*, 1966–1975, p. 174; see also David Gilson, 'Alberta Hirshheimer Burke (1906–1975), Jane Austen Society, *Collected Reports*, 1976–1985, pp. 7–8; Juliette Wells, *Everybody's Jane: Austen in the Popular Imagination*, Continuum, London and New York, 2011, pp. 34–63. Though the story is recounted that she gave the hair to the Society, in fact it was given to the Memorial Trust, which at the time ran Jane Austen's House.

DINING-ROOM GRATE

1. Elizabeth Jenkins, 'Introduction, Jane Austen Society, *Collected Reports*, 1949–65, pp. viii–x.
2. Jane Austen's House Archive, item 255, Elizabeth Jenkins to T. Edward Carpenter.
3. Virginia Woolf, *Orlando*, Vintage, London, 2004 (1928), p. 208.
4. Barbara Kirschenblatt-Gimblett, *Destination Culture: Tourism, Museums, and Heritage*, University of California Press, Berkeley CA, 1998, p. 9.

A SERMON SCRAP

1. Hampshire Record Office, Austen-Leigh Archive, MS. 23M93/86/4, cited in *Letters*, p. xvi. See also Deirdre le Faye, *A Chronology of Jane Austen and Her Family*, Cambridge University Press, Cambridge, 2006, p. 687.
2. Dorothea, Lady Charnwood, *An Autograph Collection and the Making of It*, Ernest Benn, London, 1930, p. 42.
3. *Letters*, pp. 443–4, and BL Add. MS. 70949, ff. 218, 219.
4. *Letters*, p. 217 (17 February 1813); 'Catharine Hutton, A Female Collector', *The Gentleman's Magazine: and Historical Review*, May 1846, pp. 476–7, a retrospective article. See also Kathryn Sutherland, *Why Modern Manuscripts Matter*, Oxford University Press, Oxford, 2022, pp. 98–9. For other Austen letters falling victim to division caused by the autograph craze, see *Letters*, nos 79, 80, 111, 113, 116, 117, 118, 119.
5. *Letters*, p. 231; Deirdre Le Faye, 'Updates on Jane Austen's Letters', Jane Austen Society, *Report*, 2017, pp. 26–30, with a transcription of the linen scrap at p. 29. See also Daniel Hammond, 'Lost Letter Airs Jane Austen's Dirty Linen in Public', *Daily Telegraph*, 18 February 2019.
6. In November 2019, Voewood Rare Books, Norfolk, had for sale a sermon scrap (measuring 156 × 20 mm, 6⅛ × ¾ in.) of nine words only ('every little engagement be sufficient excuse for staying away'). Included with it was a letter, dated 7 February 1871, from Austen-Leigh to a Revd J.E. Brooks: 'I send one of the only mementoes of my aunt which I can command. An

extract from a sermon which she seems to have written out of one of her brothers. I can certify that it is her hand writing.' See also Deirdre Le Faye, 'James Austen's 1814 "Sermon Scraps"', Jane Austen Society, *Report*, 2013, pp. 57–65.

CAROLINE AUSTEN, 'MY AUNT JANE AUSTEN'

1. *Memoir*, p. 169. Caroline Austen's memoir is available in full in *Memoir*, pp. 165–82.
2. The term 'biographeme' was coined by Roland Barthes in *Sade/Fourier/Loyola* (1971), trans. Richard Miller, Jonathan Cape, London, 1977, p. 9, to describe fragments of biography forming no coherent whole.
3. Samuel Johnson, *The Rambler* 68.
4. 'Printing of the Memoir by Caroline Austen', Jane Austen Society, *Collected Reports*, 1949–1965, pp. 25–6, 32.

THE COBB, LYME REGIS

1. Hallam, Lord Tennyson, *Alfred Lord Tennyson: A Memoir by His Son*, 2 vols, Macmillan, London, 1897, vol. 2, pp. 47.
2. *The Journeys of Celia Fiennes*, ed. John Hillaby, Macdonald, London, 1983, p. 30.
3. Constance Hill, *Jane Austen: Her Homes and Her Friends*, John Lane, London and New York, 1904 (1902), pp. 53–5.

CHRIS HAMMOND'S ILLUSTRATIONS, *SENSE AND SENSIBILITY*

1. Margaret Bateman, *Professional Women Upon their Professions: A Conversation*, Cambridge University Press, Cambridge, 2013 (1895), p. 20; and see Ruth Williamson, 'Hammond's Illustrated Vision of *Sense and Sensibility*', *Persuasions On-line*, vol. 43, no. 1, 2022, www.jasna.org.
2. Anne Thackeray Ritchie, *A Book of Sybils*, Smith, Elder & Co., London, 1883, p. 227.

MEMORIAL WINDOW, WINCHESTER CATHEDRAL

1. *Memoir*, p. 138.
2. *The Englishwoman's Domestic Magazine* 2, 1866, p. 238.
3. *Memoir*, p. 131.
4. Rudyard Kipling, 'The Janeites', in *Debits and Credits*, Macmillan, London, 1926, pp. 143–76. The poem was added for the 1926 edition.
5. The plaque reads 'Jane Austen Known to many by her writings, endeared to her family by the varied charms of her Character, and ennobled by Christian Faith and Piety, was born at Steventon in the county of Hampshire December 16 1775 and buried in this Cathedral July 24, 1817. "She openeth her mouth with wisdom and her tongue is the law of kindness." Proverbs 31 verse 26.'

DANISH TRANSLATION, *PRIDE AND PREJUDICE*

1. *Memoir*, p. 183.
2. A useful index of translations between 1813 and 2006 is provided in Anthony Mandal and Brian Southam (eds), *The Reception of Jane Austen in Europe*, Continuum, London, 2007, pp. xxi–xxxvi. This can be supplemented by the ongoing UNESCO Index Translationum.
3. Peter Mortensen, '"Unconditional Surrender?" Jane Austen's Reception in Denmark', in Mandal and Southam (eds), *The Reception of Jane Austen in Europe*, pp. 117–31.
4. See Hanne Maj Danielsen, 'Uncovering a Piece of Translation History', Jane Austen Society, *Report*, 2022, pp. 61–8.
5. *Jane Austen's Fiction Manuscripts*, ed. Kathryn Sutherland, 5 vols, Oxford University Press, Oxford, 2018, vol. 1, pp. 41–8.

JANE AUSTEN PLATE, CHARLESTON

1. Hana Leaper, 'The Famous Women Dinner Service: A Critical Introduction and Catalogue', *British Art Studies* 7, November 2017, https://dx.doi.org/10.17658/issn.2058–5462/issue-07/hleaper.
2. All appear in Woolf's essay 'Women and Fiction', *The Forum*, March 1929.
3. *Letters*, p. 357 and n.6.
4. Mary Hays, *Female Biography; or, Memoirs of Illustrious and Celebrated Women, of all ages and countries*, vol. 1, Richard Phillips, London, 1803, p. iv.
5. George Steiner, *After Babel: Aspects of Language and Translation*, 3rd edn, Oxford University Press, Oxford, 1998 (1975), p. 9.
6. 'Jane Austen', in *The Essays of Virginia Woolf*, ed. Andrew McNeillie, 4 vols, Hogarth Press, London, 1986–94, vol. 4, p. 149.
7. www.charleston.org.uk/stories.

REX WHISTLER'S COSTUME DESIGNS, *PRIDE AND PREJUDICE*

1. Maggie B. Gale, *West End Women: Women and the London Stage 1918–1962*, Routledge, London and New York, 1996, p. 221.
2. Rex Whistler (1905–1944). See his entry in the *Oxford Dictionary of National Biography*, https://doi-org.ezproxy-prd.bodleian.ox.ac.uk/10.1093/ref:odnb/36856.
3. Susan Sontag, 'Notes on "Camp"' (1964), in *A Susan Sontag Reader*, ed. Elizabeth Hardwick, Penguin, Harmondsworth, 1983, p. 109.
4. Eva Moore (1870–1955). See her entry in the *Oxford Dictionary of National Biography*, https://doi-org.ezproxy-prd.bodleian.ox.ac.uk/10.1093/ref:odnb/63879.
5. Mrs Hartz had purchased the six sketches in 1959(?) from dealer and bibliophile Alan G. Thomas of Bournemouth.

MR DARCY'S SHIRT

1. See essays and features under 'Jane Austen at the BBC: A Celebration in Film, TV and Radio', www.bbc.com/historyofthebbc/research/jane-austen-at-the-bbc.
2. See Kathryn Sutherland, 'Jane Austen On Screen', in Edward Copeland and Juliet McMaster (eds), *The Cambridge Companion to Jane Austen*, Cambridge University Press, Cambridge, 2011, pp. 215–31.
3. See the 100 Objects, www.bbc.com/historyofthebbc/bbc-100/100–objects.

A TEA CADDY

1. *Memoir*, p. 171.
2. *Letters*, p. 28.
3. *Lady Susan*, p. 96.
4. Recent readings of Austen family politics, like readings of *Mansfield Park*, in particular among the novels, have been heated and contentious. Devoney Looser, 'Breaking the Silence: The Austen Family's Complex Entanglements with Slavery', Jane Austen Society, *Report*, 2021, pp. 25–32, addresses succinctly both the reading and the misreading of *Mansfield Park* and provides new information on a family which 'over the course of eighty years' shifted from 'known complicity in colonial slavery to … anti-slavery activism' (p. 25). See also in the same *Report*, John Avery Jones, 'George Austen as a (nominal) Trustee of a Plantation in Antigua: The Legal Position', pp. 33–48.
5. *Letters*, p. 207 (24 January 1813).
6. As Looser makes clear ('Breaking the Silence', p. 29), Frank's disgust at slavery was not mentioned in an Austen family biography before 1906; see J.H. Hubback and Edith C. Hubback, *Jane Austen's Sailor Brothers*, John Lane, London, 1906, p. 192. For his profiting from Britain's imperial expansion, see Object 9, n.4.

GRAYSON PERRY, 'JANE AUSTEN IN E17'

1. Grayson Perry, interviewed by Alan Riding, *New York Times*, 8 December 2003, www.nytimes.com/2003/12/08/arts/transvestite-potter-wins-turner-prize-in-art.html.

LAST WORDS

1. Janet Sanders, 'Sanditon', *Times Literary Supplement*, 19 February 1925, p. 120.
2. The poem, 'When Winchester races first took their beginning', can be found in *Lady Susan*, pp. 180–81.
3. *Letters*, p. 351.
4. Louise Bourgeois, quoted in the opening of the exhibition *Structures of Existence: The Cells*, Guggenheim Museum, Bilbao, 2016.

Further reading

Austen, Jane, *Jane Austen's Letters*, ed. Deirdre Le Faye, 4th edn, Oxford University Press, Oxford, 2014.

Austen-Leigh, James Edward, *A Memoir of Jane Austen and Other Family Recollections*, ed. Kathryn Sutherland, Oxford University Press, Oxford, 2002.

Byrne, Paula, *Jane Austen and the Theatre*, Hambledon, London, 2002.

Davidson, Hilary, *Jane Austen's Wardrobe*, Yale University Press, New Haven CT and London, 2023.

Dooley, Gillian, *'She played and Sang': Jane Austen and Music*, Manchester University Press, Manchester, 2024.

Dow, Gillian, and Clare Hanson (eds), *Uses of Austen: Jane's Afterlives*, Palgrave Macmillan, London, 2012.

Gehrer, Julienne (ed.), *Martha Lloyd's Household Book*, Bodleian Library Publishing, Oxford, 2021.

Kaplan, Deborah, *Jane Austen among Women*, Johns Hopkins University Press, Baltimore MD and London, 1992.

Le Faye, Deirdre, *Jane Austen's 'Outlandish Cousin': The Life and Letters of Eliza de Feuillide*, British Library, London, 2002.

Le Faye, Deirdre, *Jane Austen: A Family Record*, Cambridge University Press, Cambridge, 2004.

Lynch, Deidre (ed.), *Janeites: Austen's Disciples and Devotees*, Princeton University Press, Princeton NJ, 2000.

Sutherland, Kathryn (ed.), *Jane Austen: Writer in the World*, Bodleian Library Publishing, Oxford, 2017.

Tomalin, Claire, *Jane Austen: A Life*, Viking, London, 1997.

Uglow, Jenny, *In These Times: Living in Britain through Napoleon's Wars 1793–1815*, Faber & Faber, London, 2014.

Watson, Nicola J., *The Author's Effects: On Writer's House Museums*, Oxford University Press, Oxford, 2020.

Wells, Juliette, *Everybody's Jane: Austen in the Popular Imagination*, Continuum, London and New York, 2011.

Image credits

1 © National Portrait Gallery, London.
2 © Jane Austen's House.
3 © Jane Austen's House.
4 Oxford, Bodleian Library, MS. Don. e. 7, pp 116–117.
5 © Jane Austen's House.
6 Hampshire Record Office: Steventon parish records, 71M82/PR3.
7 bpk/Gemäldegalerie, SMB/Jörg P. Anders, 82746, detail.
8 © Jane Austen's House.
9 © Jane Austen's House.
10 © Jane Austen's House.
11 © Jane Austen's House.
12 © Jane Austen's House.
13 Oxford, Bodleian Library, Arch. A e.108, pp. x–xi.
14 © Jane Austen's House.
15 Private collection.
16 © Jane Austen's House.
17 © Jane Austen's House.
18 © Jane Austen's House.
19 © Jane Austen's House.
    © British Library, London/Bridgeman Images.
20 © Jane Austen's House.
21 Oxford, Bodleian Library, John Johnson Collection, London Playbills Covent Garden vol. 1813–1814 (7).
22 Courtesy of John Murray.
23 Royal Collection Trust/© His Majesty King Charles III 2024, RCIN 1083626.

Index